Pd.
16/11/93

POETRY
READINGS

REVISED AND EXPANDED

MIKE TORBE and DON FRY

Hodder & Stoughton

A MEMBER OF THE HODDER HEADLINE GROUP

Every effort has been made to trace and acknowledge ownership of copyright. The Publishers will be glad to make suitable arrangements with any copyright holders whom they have been unable to contact.

The Publishers would also like to thank the following for permission to reproduce photographs and illustrations:

Llyfrgell Genedlaethol Cymru/The National Library of Wales (pages 1 and 4, bottom); Avril Lansdell (page 3, top); Barnaby's Picture Library (pages 8, 9, 15, 32 and 135); The Hulton Deutsch Collection (pages 13 and 52, centre and bottom); Robert Harding Picture Library (page 27); Don Fry (pages 39, 40 and 41); The Royal Photographic Society for 'The Bride Mrs Ewen Hay Cameron' by Julia Cameron (page 51) and 'Fading Away' by Henry Peach Robinson (page 77); Topham Picture Library (page 52, top); The Bridgeman Art Gallery for 'Mariana' by J. G. Millais (page 86) and 'Clearing in the Forest' by Caspar David Friedrich (page 108); Harmony Books and Crown Publishers Inc. for the cartoon from *The Quigmans – Love Connection!* by Buddy Hickerson (page 91); PEANUTS cartoon (page 92) reproduced by permission of United Features Syndicate, Inc.; Punch Publications (page 92).

Cover photograph of 'La Fenêtre Ouverte' by Juan Gris (1921), reproduced by kind permission of Galerie Louise Leiris, Paris.

British Library Cataloguing in Publication Data

Torbe, Mike
   Poetry Readings. – Book 1. – 2Rev.ed
   I. Title II. Fry, Donald
   821.008

   ISBN 0–340–58841–1

First published 1993
Impression number 10 9 8 7 6 5 4 3 2 1
Year   1996 1995 1994 1993

Copyright © 1993 Mike Torbe and Don Fry

All rights reserved. No part of this publication may be reproduced or transmitted in any form or by any means, electronic or mechanical, including photocopy, recording, or any information storage and retrieval system, without permission in writing from the publisher or under licence from the Copyright Licensing Agency Limited. Further details of such licences (for reprographic reproduction) may be obtained from the Copyright Licensing Agency Limited, of 90 Tottenham Court Road, London W1P 9HE.

Typeset by Wearset, Boldon, Tyne and Wear
Printed in Great Britain for the educational publishing division of Hodder & Stoughton Ltd, a division of Hodder Headline PLC, Mill Road, Dunton Green, Sevenoaks, Kent by St Edmundsbury Press, Bury St Edmunds, Suffolk.

Contents

Acknowledgements

The Publishers and authors would like to thank Sally Ingham at Settlebeck School, Sedbergh, and Libby Gurr and the English Department at the Holt School, Wokingham, for their invaluable advice on early drafts of this publication.

The Publishers would like to thank the following for permission to reproduce material in this volume:

Anvil Press Poetry for 'Foreign' by Carol Ann Duffy from *Selling Manhattan* (1987); Black Staff Press for 'Enemy Encounter' by Padraic Fiacc; 'Shadows of My Mother Against a Wall' by Helen Dunmore, reprinted by permission of Bloodaxe Books Ltd from *The Raw Garden* by Helen Dunmore (Bloodaxe Books, 1988); Carcanet Press Ltd for 'Baby Sitting', 'My Box', 'Miracle on St David's Day' and 'Marged' from *Selected Poems* by Gillian Clarke (1985), 'Buffaloes' and 'Swami Anand' from *Brunizem* by Sujatta Bhatt and two extracts from *World Without End* by Helen Thomas; André Deutsch Ltd for 'The Sniffle' by Ogden Nash, from *I Wouldn't Have Missed It*; Faber and Faber Ltd for 'Digging' from *Death of a Naturalist* by Seamus Heaney and 'The Cheetah, My Dearest Is Known Not To Cheat' by George Barker, from *Runes and Rhymes and Tunes and Chimes*; Farrar Strauss & Giroux Inc for 'One Art' by Elizabeth Bishop, from *The Complete Poems 1927–1979* © 1979, 1983 Alice Helen Methfessel; Gomer Press for 'In the Evening' by Bobi Jones, taken from *Twentieth Century Welsh Poems*; Tony Harrison for 'Bookends 1' from *Selected Poems* by Tony Harrison (published by Penguin Books); Harvill, an imprint of HarperCollins*Publishers* for 'My Boat' by Raymond Carver from *Selected Poems*; David Higham Associates for 'Rising Five' by Norman Nicholson from *The Pot Geranium* published by Faber and Faber Ltd; Hogarth Press for 'Interruption to a Journey' by Norman McCaig from *Collected Poems*; Kingfisher Books for 'The Traditional Grammarian as Poet' by Ted Hipple; James MacGibbon for permission to reprint 'Major Macross' by Stevie Smith, from *The Collected Poems of Stevie Smith*, published by Penguin Books; John Montague for 'The Trout'; Newstatesman Society for 'A Roadside Feast' by Peter Redgrove; Oxford University Press for extracts from *The Great War and Modern Memory* Paul Fussell (1975), 'House-Talk' from *Selected Poems* by Fleur Adcock (1983) and 'Ogun' from *The Arrivants* by Edward Kamau Braithwaite (1973); Evangeline Paterson for 'Dispossessed' from *Bringing the Water Hyacinth to Africa* by Evangeline Paterson, published by Taxus (1983); Penguin Books Australia Ltd for 'As Others See Us' by Basil Downing from Alan Curnow (ed.) *Penguin Book of New Zealand Poetry*; Poetry Wales Press for 'The Computer's First Proverbs *after Edwin Morgan*' from *Selected Poems* by Peter Finch; Colin Thiele for permission to reprint 'The Mushroomer', from *The Penguin Book of Modern Australian Verse*, published by Rigby Heinemann; William Stafford for his poem 'Travelling Through the Dark' from *Stories That Could Be True*; Virago Press for 'Nervous Prostration' by Anna Wickham, from *Writings of Anna Wickham* (ed. R. D. Smith) © 1984 James and George Hepburn and 'Epilogue' by Grace Nichols from *The Fat Black Woman's Poems* (1984).

Introduction

Reading poetry is rarely easy. Even experienced readers are uncertain when they read a new poem for the first time, so it is not surprising that inexperienced readers should often find poetry difficult.

This book introduces readers to different ways of reading poems to show that even poems which at first look difficult can be explored and understood. The approaches are as active as possible so that readers examine meanings in many different ways.

This book is divided into twenty units, and each unit contains:

- a core poem with its exploratory work
- an anthology
- some suggestions for assignments.

(Unit 12 (Men Talk) is different from the other units in that it contains no core poem.) The units are arranged alphabetically by the title of the core poem, and could be taken in any order that seems appropriate. They are of different lengths, depending on the poem and the approaches it suggests.

Each core poem is dealt with in a sequence of activities which have been designed to lead students through a process of making meaning. Some activities come before the poem and prepare the reader for the first reading; others come afterwards and aim to help readers understand and feel comfortable with different aspects of the poem's form, language and, above all, its meaning.

The poems in the anthologies sometimes have a theme similar to that of the main poem, sometimes are other poems by the same writer, and sometimes reflect varying aspects of the main poem in the unit. Readers can browse through the anthologies and speculate about the connections; they might also sometimes make up their own anthologies to go with the core poem.

The 'Suggestions for Assignments' offer ideas for oral and written work, which could be supplemented or replaced by a teacher's or the student's own suggestions. All assignments have to recognise the unpredictable nature of individual interests, and there should always be room for people to construct their own topics, and for individuals and groups to work at their own pace.

Students and teachers will need to decide how long to spend on a unit, and what can be done in class and what in the students' own time. Not all students, for example, will want to follow the core poem through to an assignment, and sometimes it might be better to work on the anthology later in the course.

We assume that groups have access to a library, dictionaries and other reference books to do research about poets and to find the meanings of words. Often, though, *people* are the best resource: asking questions, of each other and of helpful and informed people, will probably supply answers to many problems.

We expect that this book would represent only part of the work on poetry in a class. There would also be a general browsing through anthologies and collections, people writing their own poetry, individuals making their own choices of poems and devising assignments, visits from poets themselves to read their poems, and poetry having a place in other units of work.

1

An Arrival
Denise Levertov

AN ARRIVAL (NORTH WALES, 1897)

The orphan arrived in outlandish hat,
proud pain of new button boots.
Her moss-agate eyes
photographed views of the noonday sleepy town
no one had noticed. Nostrils flaring,
she sniffed odors of hay and stone,
              absence of Glamorgan coaldust,
and pasted her observations quickly
into the huge album of her mind.

Cousins, ready to back off like heifers
were staring:
              amazed, they received
the gold funeral sovereigns she dispensed
along with talk strange to them as a sailor's parrot.

Auntie confiscated the gold;
the mourning finery, agleam with jet,
was put by to be altered. It had been chosen
by the child herself and was thought
unsuitable. She was to be
the minister's niece, now,
not her father's daughter.
                 Alone,
she would cut her way through a new world's
graystone chapels, the steep and sideways
rockface cottages climbing
mountain streets,

enquiring, turning things over
in her heart,
              weeping only in rage or when
the choirs in their great and dark and
golden glory broke forth and the hills
skipped like lambs.

▷ Choose from the poem words or lines that seem to be captions for the
   photographs on the previous pages.

▷ What would the people in North Wales think about the orphan girl?
   Construct a dialogue between the aunt and an imaginary neighbour
   in which they discuss the newcomer.

▷ '. . . she . . . pasted her observations quickly
into the huge album of her mind.'

Imagine you are the girl, now a woman, telling your daughter the
story about your own childhood. Write what you might say about
two or three of the following:

- her arrival in North Wales

- losing the 'mourning finery'

- being 'the minister's niece, now,/ not her father's daughter'

- 'turning things over/ in her heart'

- 'weeping . . . in rage'

- the choirs

Use what's in the poem, but add your own ideas by imagining what
the full story might have been.

▷ As a minister's niece, the girl would have gone regularly to chapel
and become familiar with the Bible.
    Here is Psalm 114 from the Authorised Version of the Bible. How
has it found its way into the poem?

PSALM 114

When Israel went out of Egypt, the
house of Jacob from a people of
strange language;
    Judah was his sanctuary, *and* Israel
his dominion.
    The sea saw *it*, and fled: Jordan was
driven back.
    The mountains skipped like rams,
and the little hills like lambs.
    What *ailed* thee, O thou sea, that thou
fleddest? thou Jordan, *that* thou wast
driven back?
    Yet mountains, *that* ye skipped like
rams; *and* ye little hills, like lambs?
    Tremble, thou earth, at the presence
of the Lord, at the presence of the God
of Jacob;
    Which turned the rock *into* a stand-
ing water, the flint into a fountain of
waters.

Anthology: Poems by Denise Levertov _____

THE INSTANT

'We'll go out before breakfast, and get
some mushrooms,' says my mother.

Early, early: the sun
risen, but hidden in mist

the square house left behind
sleeping, filled with sleepers;

up the dewy hill, quietly, with baskets.

Mushrooms firm, cold;
      tussocks of dark grass, gleam of webs,
turf soft and cropped. Quiet and early. And no valley,

no hills: clouds about our knees, tendrils
of cloud in our hair. Wet scrags
of wool caught in barbed wire, gorse
looming, without scent.
                Then ah! suddenly
the lifting of it, the mist rolls
    quickly away, and far, far –

'Look!' she grips me, 'It is
        Eryri!
          It's Snowdon, fifty
    miles away!' – the voice
a wave rising to Eryri,
falling.
    Snowdon, home
of eagles, resting place of
Merlin, core of Wales.

      Light
graces the mountainhead
for a lifetime's look, before the mist
    draws in again.

THE QUARRY POOL

Between town and the
old house, an inn –
the Half-Way House.
So far one could ride, I remember,

the rest was an uphill walk,
a mountain lane with
steep banks and sweet
hedges, half walls of

gray rock. Looking
again at this looking-glass face
unaccountably changed in a week,
three weeks, a month,

I think without thinking of
Half-Way House. Is it
the thought that this far
I've driven at ease, as in a bus,

a country bus where one could talk to the driver?
Now on foot towards the village;
the dust clears, silence
draws in around one. I hear
the rustle and hum of the fields: alone.

It must be the sense
of essential solitude that chills me
looking into my eyes.
I should remember

the old house at the walk's ending,
a square place with a courtyard,
granaries, netted strawberry-beds,
a garden that was many

gardens, each one
a world hidden from the
next by leaves, enlaced trees,
fern-hairy walls, gilly-flowers.

I should see, making
a strange face at myself,
nothing to fear in the thought of
Half-Way House –

the place one got down
to walk —. What is
this shudder, this
dry mouth?

Think, please, of the quarry pool,
the garden's furthest
garden, of your childhood's
joy in its solitude.

Suggestions for assignments

1 Write answers to these questions about the poems in this unit:
The Instant
(The mother in 'The Instant' was the child in 'An Arrival'.)
   Why is it that the moment in which she saw Snowdon is so imporatnt
now to the writer?
   Do you feel that the moment was as significant then to the mother as
it is now to the daughter?
The Quarry Pool
What do you feel you need to know in order to understand this poem
fully?

2 What do the poems tell you about the things that remain from
childhood? Work with someone else or with a small group, and make
notes about: places that stay in people's memory, the idea of revisiting
places, old photographs, memorable moments and any other aspects of
the poems that seem relevant.
   Write a piece, either individually or collectively, that summarises
what you have talked about.

2

As the Team's Head-Brass
Edward Thomas

It is 1917, in Gloucestershire. A ploughman is ploughing a field which has lain fallow. There is a wood along one side of it, and a tree has fallen at the opposite side from the wood. Sitting on the fallen tree is a man in uniform, who watches the ploughman, and also sees two people just going into the wood. The horses pulling the plough have head-brasses which the soldier sees flash in the sun as they turn at the end of the furrow and come back up towards him.

When the plough turns near the soldier, the ploughman rests and chats to him. Then he sets off again, with the earth turning over away from the blade of the plough-share.

The ploughman explains how the tree fell. The soldier asks when they'll move it, the ploughman answers, and so they chat, during the one minute out of every ten that the plough is resting near the soldier. The soldier speaks first and the conversation turns to the war. In France, men are dying, guns are firing, trenches are being dug, and the Great War is destroying the youth of Europe. But here, the soldier takes his last look at the peaceful scene before he leaves it.

Here now is the poem, 'As the Team's Head-Brass'. Edward Thomas, the poet, who is the soldier in the poem, did go to war. He was killed in Flanders in 1917.

AS THE TEAM'S HEAD-BRASS

As the team's head-brass flashed out on the turn
The lovers disappeared into the wood.
I sat among the boughs of the fallen elm
That strewed the angle of the fallow, and
Watched the plough narrowing a yellow square
Of charlock. Every time the horses turned
Instead of treading me down, the ploughman leaned
Upon the handles to say or ask a word,
About the weather, next about the war.
Scraping the share he faced towards the wood,
And screwed along the furrow till the brass flashed once more.
             The blizzard felled the elm whose crest
I sat in, by a woodpecker's round hole,
The ploughman said. 'When will they take it away?'
'When the war's over.' So the talk began —
One minute and an interval of ten,
A minute more and the same interval.
'Have you been out?' 'No.' 'And don't want to, perhaps?'
'If I could only come back again, I should.
I could spare an arm. I shouldn't want to lose
A leg. If I should lose my head, why, so,
I should want nothing more. . . . Have many gone
From here?' 'Yes.' 'Many lost?' 'Yes, a good few.
Only two teams work on the farm this year.
One of my mates is dead. The second day
In France they killed him. It was back in March,
The very night of the blizzard too. Now if
He had stayed here we should have moved the tree.'
'And I should not have sat here. Everything
Would have been different. For it would have been
Another world.' 'Ay, and a better, though
If we could see all all might seem good.' Then
The lovers came out of the wood again:
The horses started and for the last time
I watched the clods crumble and topple over
After the ploughshare and the stumbling team.

10

▷ Make a sketch or diagram of the scene in the poem, showing the field, the tree, the wood, the characters, the movement of the ploughing team, and so on.

▷ Think of the poem as bringing together three worlds:

- the world of the soldier

- the world of the ploughman

- the world of war

Make a copy of this diagram big enough for you to write in the circles.

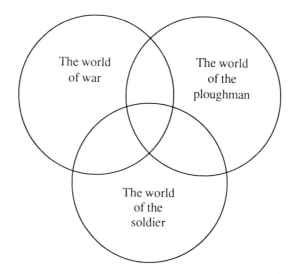

Where in this diagram would you place these elements from the poem:

- the fallen tree

- the ploughman's mate

- the blizzard

- the lovers

- the ploughing

Which did you find the hardest to decide about?

▷ Explain why you put the elements where you did. You could do this either as a piece of writing, or as notes for a presentation to the rest of the class.

Anthology _____

20th. Stiff deep mud all the way up and shelled as we started. Telegraph Hill as quiet as if only rabbits lived there. I took revolver and left this diary behind in case. For it is very exposed and only a few Cornwalls and MGC [Machine Gun Corps] about. But Hun shelled chiefly over our heads into Beaurains all night – like starlings returning 20 or 30 a minute. Horrible flap of 5.9 a little along the trench. Rain and mud and I've to stay till I am relieved tomorrow. Had not brought warm clothes or enough food and had no shelter, nor had telephonists. Shelled all night. But the M.G.C. boy gave me tea. I've no bed. I leant against wall of trench. I got up and looked over. I stamped up and down. I tried to see patrol out. Very light – the only sign of Hun on Telegraph Hill, though 2 appeared and were sniped at. A terribly long night and cold. Not relieved till 8. Telephonists out repairing line since 4 on the morning of the . . .

21st. At last 260 relieved us. Great pleasure to be going back to sleep and rest. No Man's Land like Goodwood Racecourse with engineers swarming over it and making a road between shell holes full of blood-stained water and beer bottles among barbed wire. Larks singing as they did when we went up in dark and were shelled. Now I hardly felt as if a shell could hurt, though several were thrown about near working parties. Found letters from Helen, Eleanor and Julian. Had lunch, went to bed at 2 intending to get up to tea, but slept till 6.30 on the [22nd]

(*Diary of Edward Thomas*)

Since dawn was the favourite time for launching attacks, at the order to stand-to everyone, officers, men, forward artillery obser-vers, visitors, mounted the fire-step, weapon ready, and peered toward the German line. When it was almost full light and clear that the Germans were not going to attack that morning, everyone 'stood down' and began preparing breakfast in small groups. The rations of tea, bread, and bacon, brought up in sandbags during the night, were broken out. The bacon was fried in mess-tin lids over small, and if possible smokeless, fires.

(*The Great War and Modern Memory* by Paul Fussell)

The agony of the men being shelled began well before the explosion. The skilled ear picked out each gun, noted its calibre, the path of its shell and the likely explosion point. The small field gun went off with a crack like a fat man hitting a golf ball. The shell took off like a jet plane and arrived with a screaming shriek. A keen pair of eyes might pick out the fifteen-foot gunflash, blinding even as a flashlight in daytime. The medium artillery piece sounded like a giant newspaper being torn, its shell a farmcart coming down a steep hill with its brakes on. The heavy gun rapped a man's head with a heavy cane then rolled in a leisurely arc across the sky, a man on a bicycle whistling slowly and pensively. For a time the listener felt he could run beside it. Then it speeded up like an express train rushing down a tunnel. Shells passing over woods

13

and valleys echoed. Shells falling in enclosed places came with a double bang and no warning. A near miss would whistle or roar, with debris raining down long after the burst. The strain of listening for all these sounds did something to the brain. A man could never be rid of them. [. . .]

If a man were unstable and ill-suited to war, whatever he might consciously think, a shellburst would most effectively prick the lie. Drury remembered an eighteen-year-old trembling for twenty-four hours after a dud dropped ten yards from him.

(*Ibid.*)

Birds gave pleasure to most. The bared soil rich in nitrates from shelling and free from the attention of farmers produced a vast crop of plants, particularly of cornflowers and poppies. Attracting insects, these flowers brought birds in their wake. A letter in the *Daily Express* (27 October 1918) noted sixty species within two miles of Péronne. The resilience of these birds gave men hope, and the press published a succession of letters, like *The Times* (2 March 1916), which noted a nightingale nesting in the front line at Hooge. A nightingale sang on the Ancre three days after a mustard attack (16 June 1918) with comment from the *Guardian*. The *Daily Express* (5 May 1916) published a letter describing a blackbird laying four eggs and bringing up its young in the guts of a heavy gun in constant use. However harsh the barrage, birds never missed the dawn chorus.

(*Death's Men* by Denis Winter)

We had a march of 3 miles over shelled road then nearly 3 along a flooded trench. After that we came to where the trenches had been blown flat out and had to go over the top. It was of course dark, too dark, and the ground was not mud, not sloppy mud, but an octopus of sucking clay, 3, 4, and 5 feet deep, relieved only by craters full of water. Men have been known to drown in them. Many stuck in the mud & only got on by leaving their waders, equipment, and in some cases their clothes.

(*Diary of Wilfred Owen*)

Today the Somme is a peaceful but sullen place, unforgetting and unforgiving. The people, who work largely at raising vegetables and grains, are 'correct' but not friendly. To wander now over the fields destined to extrude their rusty metal fragments for centuries is to appreciate in the most intimate way the permanent reverberations of July, 1916. When the air is damp you can smell rusted iron everywhere, even though you see only wheat and barley. The farmers work the fields without joy. They collect the duds, shell-casings, fuses, and shards of old barbed wire as the plow unearths them and stack them in the corners of their fields. Some

15

of the old barbed wire, both British and German, is used for fencing. Many of the shell craters are still there, though smoothed out and grown over. The mine craters are too deep to be filled and remain much as they were. When the sun is low in the afternoon, on the gradual slopes of the low hills you see the traces of the zig-zag of trenches. Many farmhouses have out in back one of the little British wooden huts that used to house soldiers well behind the lines; they make handy toolsheds. Lurking in every spot of undergrowth just off the beaten track are eloquent little things: rusted buckles, rounds of corroded small-arms ammunition, metal tabs from ammunition boxes, bits of Bully tin, buttons.

(*The Great War and Modern Memory*)

Thomas's wife wrote about herself ('Jenny') and Thomas. Here are two extracts from her book.

The days had passed in restless energy for us both. He had sawn up a big tree that had blown down at our very door, and chopped the branches into logs, the children all helping. The children loved being with him, for though he was stern in making them build up the logs properly, and use the tools in the right way, they were not resentful of this, but tried to win his rare praise and imitate his skill. Indoors he packed his kit and polished his accoutrement. He loved a good piece of leather, and his Sam Browne and high trenchboots shone with a deep clear lustre. The brass, too, reminded him of the brass ornaments we had often admired when years ago we had lived on a farm and knew every detail of a plough team's harness. We all helped with the buttons and buckles and badges to turn him out the smart officer it was his pride to be. For he entered into this soldiering which he hated in just the same spirit of thoroughness of which I have spoken before. We talked, as we polished, of those past days: 'Do you remember when Jingo, the grey leader of the team, had colic, and Turner the ploughman led her about Blooming Meadow for hours, his eyes streaming with tears because he thought she was going to die? And how she would only eat the hay from Blooming Meadow, and not the coarse hay that was grown in Sixteen Acre Meadow for the cows? And do you remember Turner's whip which he carried over his shoulder when he led Darling and Chestnut and Jingo out to the plough? It had fourteen brass bands on the handle, one for every year of his service on the farm.' So we talked of old times that the children could remember.

(*World Without End* by Helen Thomas)

'And here are my poems. I've copied them all out in this book for you, and the last of all is for you. I wrote it last night, but don't read it now. . . . It's still freezing. The ground is like iron, and more snow has fallen. The children will come to the station with me; and now I must be off.'

We were alone in my room. He took me in his arms, holding me tightly to him, his face white, his eyes full of a fear I had never seen before. My arms were round his neck. 'Beloved, I love you,' was all I could say. 'Jenny, Jenny, Jenny,' he said, 'remember that, whatever happens, all is well between us for ever and ever.' And hand in hand we went downstairs and out to the children, who were playing in the snow.

A thick mist hung everywhere, and there was no sound except, far away in the valley, a train shunting. I stood at the gate watching him go; he turned back to wave until the mist and the hill hid him. I heard his old call coming up to me: 'Coo-ee!' he called. 'Coo-ee!' I answered, keeping my voice strong to call again. Again through the muffled air came his 'Coo-ee'. And again went my answer like an echo. 'Coo-ee' came fainter next time with the hill between us, but my 'Coo-ee' went out of my lungs strong to pierce to him as he strode away from me. 'Coo-ee!' So faint now, it might be only my own call flung back from the thick air and muffling snow. I put my hands up to my mouth to make a trumpet, but no sound came. Panic seized me, and I ran through the mist and the snow to the top of the hill, and stood there a moment dumbly, with straining eyes and ears. There was nothing but the mist and the snow and the silence of death.

Then with leaden feet which stumbled in a sudden darkness that overwhelmed me I groped my way back to the empty house.

(*Ibid.*)

Suggestions for assignments ────────────

1 Here is the beginning of the conversation in the poem printed as though it were a page from a play:

SOLDIER: When will they take it away?
PLOUGHMAN: When the war's over.
             (There is a pause during which the plough moves away and then returns.)

Work with another person and try different ways of acting out the conversation between the soldier and the ploughman.

As you decide how they would speak, you will have to think of their state of mind.

Remember that the way people feel sometimes comes out in the way they say things, but sometimes what they really feel isn't shown.

What are you going to do about the pauses?

Now go back to the poem on page 10.

Decide how the two of you will read the poem aloud. When you are ready, record or perform your reading to others.

2 The poem tells you what the soldier sees, what he says, and what he does. What is he feeling though? What is he thinking?

Think of yourself as the soldier. Describe what he sees, says and does in the course of the poem, and add to it your description of what he feels and thinks. Use 'I' and write as though the events are happening now.

3 Use the poem, and all the anthology material. Imagine one of these scenes:

(a) It's dawn, and the soldier in the poem is at the Front.

(b) The soldier has returned home and revisits the place in the poem.

(c) The wife receives a letter from the Front.

You could write in any of these forms:

- a conversation

- a diary

- a story

- a letter or an exchange of letters

- a poem

- memoirs written many years later

3

Book Ends
Tony Harrison

BOOK ENDS

Baked the day she suddenly dropped dead
we chew it slowly that last apple pie.

Shocked into sleeplessness you're scared of bed.
We never could talk much, and now don't try.

You're like book ends, the pair of you, she'd say,
Hog that grate, say nothing, sit, sleep, stare . . .

The 'scholar' me, you, worn out on poor pay,
only our silence made us seem a pair.

Not as good for staring in, blue gas,
too regular each bud, each yellow spike.

A night you need my company to pass
and she not here to tell us we're alike!

Your life's all shattered into smithereens.

Back in our silences and sullen looks,
for all the Scotch we drink, what's still between 's
not the thirty or so years, but books, books, books.

▷ Work with a partner. Write out each pair of lines. Underneath each pair, write out:

- what you think it means

- what it makes you think of

  If you have any questions you can't answer yourselves, note them down.
  Share what you have written with another pair. Discuss together any questions you have collected.

▷ In what ways are the two people in the poem close to each other? What keeps them together? What keeps them apart?
  Write your own answers to these questions; and then share what you have written with the other people in your group.
  As a group, produce answers to the questions: you might include parts of what individuals have written, or you might decide to write a new group version.

▷ The son is silent with his father but eloquent in the poem.

'We never could talk much and now don't try'

'. . . in our silences and sullen looks'

Why is he able to talk about his feelings in the poem but not when he is actually with his father?

▷ What does Tony Harrison feel at the end of the poem?

'. . . what's still between 's . . . books, books, books'

What does this mean?

Anthology ———————————————————————

IN THE EVENING

In the evening by the fire my father comes surging back,
Some things we once did together, and I so often
Unkind. And then his considerate courtesy takes form
And draws my heart beneath his proud and simple wing.

When the great gap left by his loss grew wider
I did not know he would stay in me, so final was his going,
And would rush to my head as if he were stretching at home
In the evening by the fire, his feet on the shelf of my mind.

Behind the world's back, in the evening by the fire
His love comes wandering down, see, it returns.
It drops through my veins to switch their electric on
To light my recollection with the days that were so delightful;
And I too walk over to the dusk of some day
Towards a hearth of all rebinding, a storehouse of each love.

Bobi Jones

I made myself an expert
in farewells. An unexpected November
shut the door in my face:

I crashed, a glasshouse
hit by the stone of Father's death.
At the burning ghat

relations stood like exclamation points.
The fire stripped his unwary body
of the last shred of family likeness.

I am my father now.
The lines of my hands
hold the fine compass of his going:

I shall follow. And after me,
my unborn son, through the eye of this needle
of forgetfulness.

R Parthasarathy

DAD

Your old hat hurts me, and those black
    fat raisins you liked to press into
my palm from your soft heavy hand:
    I see you staggering back up the path
with sacks of potatoes from some local farm,
    fresh eggs, flowers. Every day I grieve

for your great heart broken and you gone.
    You loved to watch the trees. This year
you did not see their Spring.
    The sky was freezing over the fen
as on that somewhere secretly appointed day
    you beached: cold, white-faced, shivering.

What happened, old bull, my loyal
    hoarse-voiced warrior? The hammer
blow that stopped you in your track
    and brought you to a hospital monitor
could not destroy your courage
    to the end you were
uncowed and unconcered with pleasing anyone.

I think of you now as once again safely
    at my mother's side, the earth as
chosen as a bed, and feel most sorrow for
    all that was gentle in
my childhood buried there
    already forfeit, now forever lost.

Elaine Feinstein

MAKE BELIEVE

Say I were not sixty,
say you weren't near-hundred,
say you were alive.
Say my verse was read
in some distant country,
and say you were idly turning the pages:

The blood washed from your shirt,
the tears from your eyes,
the earth from your bones;
neither missing since 1940,
nor dead as reported later
by a friend of a friend of a friend . . .

Quite dapper you stand in that bookshop
and chance upon my clues.

That is why at sixty
when some publisher askes me
for biographical details,
I still carefully give
the year of my birth,
the name of my hometown:

GERDA MAYER born '27, in Karlsbad,
Czechoslovakia . . . write to me, father.

Gerda Mayer

NOTE: The author's father, Arnold Stein, escaped
from the German concentration camp in Nisko in
1939, fled to Russian-occupied Lemberg/Lwow,
and then disappeared in the summer of 1940. It is
thought he may have died in a Russian camp.

Suggestions for assignments _____

1 If you wrote about the line in Tony Harrison's poem ('What's still between 's . . .'), then you began to think about the relationship between one man and his father. 'Between us' might mean both 'what links us' and 'what separates us'.

Each of the poets thinks about the relationship with his or her father and how he or she feels about it. Write about some, or all, of the poems in the anthology with 'Between us' as your theme.

2 Talk to an older person about his or her memories of being with his or her father. The poems in this unit give you some ideas for starting points.

Write a piece – which could be a poem, story or some other form – based on what this older person has told you and what you feel about it. You could include what you have read here.

4

Buffaloes
Sujata Bhatt

▷ The lines that follow are about a young woman. Work together and
list as much as you can about her:

- what has happened to her

- where she lives

- how she feels

- what her dreams are

> The young widow
> walks from tree to tree,
> newly opened leaves brush damp sweet smells
> across her face. The infant's mouth sleeps
> against her breast. Dreams stuck
> inside her chest twitch,
> as she watches the buffaloes pass
> too close to her house, up the steep road
> to the dairy.

▷ Here is some more information about her from earlier in the poem.

> The young widow
> thinks she should have burned on
> her husband's funeral pyre.
> She could not, for her mother-in-law
> insisted she raise the only son
> of her only son.
> The young widow sits outside
> in the garden overlooking a large pond.
> Out of the way, still untouchable, she suckles
> her three-week-old son
> and thinks she could live
> for those hungry lips; live to let him grow
> bigger than herself.

Reread your earlier list and adjust what you said there, adding any more information about the woman that you have discovered.

BUFFALOES

The young widow
thinks she should have burned on
her husband's funeral pyre.
She could not, for her mother-in-law
insisted she raise the only son
of her only son.
The young widow sits outside
in the garden overlooking a large pond.
Out of the way, still untouchable, she suckles
her three-week-old son
and thinks she could live
for those hungry lips; live to let him grow
bigger than herself. Her dreams lie
lazily swishing their tails
in her mind like buffaloes
dozing, some with only nostrils showing
in a muddy pond.

Tails switch
to keep fat flies away,
and horns, as long as a man's hand, or longer,
keep the boys, and their pranks away.
It is to the old farmer's tallest son
they give their warm yellowish milk.
He alone approaches: dark-skinned and naked
except for a white turban, a white loincloth.
He joins them in the pond,
greets each one with love:
'my beauty', 'my pet' –
slaps water on their broad flanks
splashes more water on their dusty backs.
Ears get scratched, necks rubbed,
drowsy faces are splashed awake.
Now he prods them out of the mud
out of the water, begging loudly
'Come my beauty, come my pet, let us go!'
And the pond shrinks back
as the wide black buffaloes rise.
The young widow
walks from tree to tree,
newly opened leaves brush damp sweet smells
across her face. The infant's mouth sleeps
against her breast. Dreams stuck
inside her chest twitch,
as she watches the buffaloes pass
too close to her house, up the steep road
to the dairy. The loud loving voice
of the farmer's son holds them steady
without the bite of any stick or whip.

▷ This is a commonplace scene that is repeated in this place often. Why is it especially important to the young widow today?

▷ What are her dreams about (lines 13–17 and 42–3)?

▷ Imagine a time after the end of this poem, when the young widow has returned home with her baby, and is talking to someone about what has happened to her today, and how she feels now. Write your own piece that begins

The young widow
says –

Anthology

THAT DISTANCE APART
(Part V)

She, my little foreigner
no longer familiar with my womb

kicking her language of living
somewhere past stalking her first words

she is six years old today
I am twenty-five; we are only

that distance apart yet
time has fossilised

prehistoric time is easier
I can imagine dinosaurs

more vivid than my daughter
dinosaurs do not hurt my eyes

nor make me old so terribly old
we are land sliced and torn.

Jackie Kay

WHEN I HEARD THE LEARN'D
ASTRONOMER

When I heard the learn'd astronomer,
When the proofs, the figures, were ranged in columns
   before me,
When I was shown the charts and diagrams, to add, divide,
   and measure them,
When I sitting heard the astronomer where he lectured
   with much applause in the lecture-room,

How soon unaccountable I became tired and sick,
Till rising and gliding out I wander'd off by myself,
In the mystical moist night-air, and from time to time,
Look'd up in perfect silence at the stars.

Walt Whitman

THE COMING OF GOOD LUCK

So good luck came, and on my roof did light,
Like noiseless snow, or as the dew of night:
Not all at once, but gently, as the trees
Are by the sunbeams tickled by degrees.

Robert Herrick

Suggestions for assignments

1 Take the first draft material you produced in the last task on
'Buffaloes' – writing about 'The young widow says –'. Work it up into a
more polished and final piece which would satisfy readers even if they
had not read the poem.

2 Make a presentation on paper which links the poems together. Put
copies of the three anthology poems in the centre of the paper. On one
side write something which describes the feelings at the centre of the
poem. It may help to write this if you begin with 'I realise that . . .' or 'I
feel . . .' or 'I find that . . .'.
   On the other side of each poem write something which describes
similar feelings in 'Buffaloes'. You might be able to use some of the
writing you have already done on the poem.

5

Digging
Seamus Heaney

▷ Write the word 'digging' in the middle of a piece of paper. Work together and write down whatever comes into your mind about the word. Write your suggestions around the paper in whatever way seems best.

'Digging' was Seamus Heaney's first published poem. The poet hears the sound of a spade, as his father works in the garden outside the room where the poet is writing. He remembers his own childhood twenty years ago, and his father working in the potato field. 'By God,' he thinks, 'the old man could handle a spade, just like his old man' (i.e. his own grandfather). He remembers taking milk to his grandfather, while he was cutting turf for burning.

DIGGING

Between my finger and my thumb
The squat pen rests; snug as a gun.

Under my window, a clean rasping sound
When the spade sinks into gravelly ground:
My father, digging. I look down

Till his straining rump among the flowerbeds
Bends low, comes up twenty years away
Stooping in rhythm through potato drills
Where he was digging.

The coarse boot nestled on the lug, the shaft
Against the inside knee was levered firmly.
He rooted out tall tops, buried the bright edge deep
To scatter new potatoes that we picked
Loving their cool hardness in our hands.

By God, the old man could handle a spade.
Just like his old man.

My grandfather cut more turf in a day
Than any other man on Toner's bog.
Once I carried him milk in a bottle
Corked sloppily with paper. He straightened up
To drink it, then fell to right away

Nicking and slicing neatly, heaving sods
Over his shoulder, going down and down
For the good turf. Digging.

The cold smell of potato mould, the squelch and slap
Of soggy peat, the curt cuts of an edge
Through living roots awaken in my head.
But I've no spade to follow men like them.

Between my finger and my thumb
The squat pen rests.
I'll dig with it.

▷ There are three generations mentioned in the poem. Mark on a copy of the poem the parts which are about each of them. One way is to put different coloured boxes round the various bits.

▷ Make a note of when the words 'dig' or 'digging' are used in the poem, and which lines they are in.

   Who is doing the 'digging' in each case?

▷ Go back to the word web you made for 'digging'. Now that you know that the word is the title of this poem, cross out the words that no longer seem to fit.

   What different meanings does the word 'digging' have in the poem?

▷ On another piece of paper, draw a box and write in it one sentence about the poem. It could be a question you want to ask, a statement you want to make about the poem's meaning to you, or something it has made you remember or think about.

   Exchange papers within your group, and write comments on each others' versions.

   When you get your own paper back, revise or add to your original boxed statement in the light of what other people have said, and what you have read.

Seamus Heaney has written that, when he was writing the poem 'Digging', he remembered something said by an old roadman he knew as a child. He would pass the man on his way to school and make himself late by talking to him. The man's job was to cut back the brambles and tidy up the verge. Heaney writes:

> Leaning on his spade, this man once said to me: 'The pen's easily handled. It's a lot lighter than the spade. Aye, boy, it's lighter than the spade, I'm telling you.'

▷ *'But I've no spade . . .'*
   Why does he say that? Is he ashamed of it, or pleased and relieved?

OGUN

My uncle made chairs, tables, balanced doors on, dug out
coffins, smoothing the white wood out

with plane and quick sandpaper until
it shone like his short-sighted glasses.

The knuckles of his hands were sil-
vered knobs of nails hit, hurt and flat-

tened out with blast of heavy hammer. He was knock-knee'd, flat-
footed and his clip clop sandals slapped across the concrete

flooring of his little shop where canefield mulemen and a fleet
of Bedford lorry drivers dropped in to scratch themselves and talk.

There was no shock of wood, no beam
of light mahogany his saw teeth couldn't handle.

When shaping squares for locks, a key hole
care tapped rat tat tat upon the handle

of his humpbacked chisel. Cold
world of wood caught fire as he whittled: rectangle

window frames, the intersecting x of fold-
ing chairs, triangle

trellises, the donkey
box-cart in its squeaking square.

But he was poor and most days he was hungry.
Imported cabinets with mirrors, formica table

tops, spine-curving chairs made up of tubes, with hollow
steel-like bird bones that sat on rubber ploughs,

thin beds, stretched not on boards, but blue high-tensioned cables,
were what the world preferred.

And yet he had a block of wood that would have baffled them.
With knife and gimlet care he worked away at this on Sundays,

explored its knotted hurts, cutting his way
along its yellow whorls until his hands could feel

how it had swelled and shivered, breathing air,
its weathered green burning to rings of time,

its contoured grain still tuned to roots and water.
And as he cut, he heard the creak of forests:

green lizard faces gulped, grey memories with moth
eyes watched him from their shadows, soft

liquid tendrils leaked among the flowers
and a black rigid thunder he had never heard within his hammer

came stomping up the trunks. And as he worked within his shattered
Sunday shop, the wood took shape: dry shuttered

eyes, slack anciently everted lips, flat
ruined face, eaten by pox, ravaged by rat

and woodworm, dry cistern mouth, cracked
gullet crying for the desert, the heavy black

enduring jaw; lost pain, lost iron;
emerging woodwork image of his anger.

Edward Kamau Brathwaite

SWAMI ANAND

In Kosbad during the monsoons
there are so many shades of green
your mind forgets other colours.

At that time
I am seventeen, and have just started
to wear a sari every day.
Swami Anand is eighty-nine
                and almost blind
His thick glasses don't seem to work,
they only magnify his cloudy eyes.
Mornings he summons me
        from the kitchen
and I read to him until lunch time.

One day he tells me
'you can read your poems now'
I read a few, he is silent.
Thinking he's asleep, I stop.
But he says, 'continue'.
I begin a long one
in which the Himalayas rise
                as a metaphor.
Suddenly I am ashamed
to have used the Himalayas like this,
ashamed to speak of my imaginary mountains
to a man who walked through
            the ice and snow of Gangotri
                    barefoot
a man who lived close to Kangchenjanga
        and Everest clad only in summer cotton.
I pause to apologize
but he says 'just continue'.

Later, climbing through
        the slippery green hills of Kosbad,
Swami Anand does not need to lean
on my shoulder or his umbrella.
I prod him for suggestions,
ways to improve my poems.
He is silent a long while,
then, he says
        'there is nothing I can tell you
                except continue.'

Sujata Bhatt

Suggestions for assignments —————————————

1 One concern of the poems in this section is memories about events in the poets' lives, concerning people from an older generation whom the poets respect, and from whom they learned something important.

   Write about your own memories of some older person who seems now to be important to you.

Notice what the three poems do:

- They are very precise about the place.

- They give physical details of clothing, tools and belongings.

- They give strong pictures of the people. (You might want to use photographs of the person you are writing about.)

- They make it very clear what the older people were good at.

2 Suppose we said to each of the poets: Why have you written about these people? Examples of the questions you could ask are:

- What is it about your father and grandfather/your uncle/the Swami that you especially remember?

- Do you feel you are different from them?

- What difference did they make to your life and your work?

- What did you mean when you said 'as he cut [my uncle] heard the creak of forests'?

- How did you feel when the Swami said 'There is nothing I can tell you except continue'?

- What do you three poets feel you have in common?

Some of the ways you could organise this would be to:

- work on your own and write the answers as a report of an interview

- work with a partner and prepare an interview which you could record or present to the class

- work as a whole class, with each poet played by a different person

The oral part of this assignment could lead to written work which could either be a transcript of the interview, or an essay.

6

During Wind and Rain
Thomas Hardy

T hese photographs are from a family's album. They all come
from the same period. Is there anything in the photographs that
reminds you of pictures of your own family, or are they very
different?

Here are four memories of a Victorian family.

1 The family is working together in the garden, clearing and tidying, and making somewhere to sit in the shade:

> They clear the creeping moss –
> Elders and juniors – aye,
> Making the pathways neat
>   And the garden gay;
> And they build a shady seat. . . .

2 In the summer, they breakfast outside. The guinea fowl they keep as pets come up to them for food. In the distance, they can just see the sea:

> They are blithely breakfasting all –
> Men and maidens – yea,
> Under the summer tree,
>   With a glimpse of the bay,
> While pet fowl come to the knee. . . .

3 Another memory is of moving house, with all the furniture out on the lawn, waiting to be loaded on to carts:

> They change to a high new house,
> He, she, all of them – aye,
> Clocks and carpets and chairs
>   On the lawn all day
> And brightest things that are theirs. . . .

4 In the evenings, by candlelight, they all join in singing their favourite songs in harmony, while one person plays the piano:

> They sing their dearest songs –
> He, she, all of them – yea,
> Treble and tenor and bass,
>   And one to play;
> With the candles mooning each face. . . .

▷ Reread each of the four memories. Try picturing each of the memories: you might find it helpful to draw them as though they are photographs in their own frame.
   Put them in some sort of sequence – time of day, time of the year, time of life . . . Which seems the best sequence?

The poem is in four verses, one for each memory. The memories that
you have seen end with dots (. . .) meaning that both the memory and
the verse are incomplete.

Here are the last two lines of the poem: rain runs down the family
gravestone:

> Ah, no; the years, the years;
> Down their carved names the raindrop ploughs.

The poem is called 'During Wind and Rain' and is given over the page
as Hardy wrote it.

DURING WIND AND RAIN

They sing their dearest songs –
He, she, all of them, yea,
Treble and tenor and bass,
    And one to play;
With the candles mooning each face. . . .
    Ah, no; the years O!
How the sick leaves reel down in throngs!

They clear the creeping moss –
Elders and juniors – aye,
Making the pathways neat
    And the garden gay;
And they build a shady seat. . . .
    Ah, no; the years, the years;
See, the white storm-birds wing across!

They are blithely breakfasting all –
Men and maidens – yea,
Under the summer tree,
    With a glimpse of the bay,
While pet fowl come to the knee. . . .
    Ah no; the years O!
And the rotten rose is ript from the wall.

They change to a high new house,
He, she, all of them – aye,
Clocks and carpets and chairs
    On the lawn all day,
And brightest things that are theirs. . . .
    Ah, no; the years, the years;
Down their carved names the rain-drop ploughs.

▷ The wind strips the trees, whirls birds across the sky, and tears down the dead rose. Four times we are reminded of 'the years' passing.

Go back to the pictures you drew of the memories. Add something to them that represents how your view of them has changed now that you have seen the whole poem.

▷ Work in pairs, and look at the ways in which the poem is patterned. For example:

- look at the sixth line in each verse

- look at the second line in each verse

- look at the words that rhyme with 'play'

Make up some directions of your own that would help other people to discover patterns in the poem.

Anthology: Poems by Thomas Hardy ──────

'AH, ARE YOU DIGGING ON MY GRAVE?'

'Ah, are you digging on my grave,
　　My loved one? – planting rue?'
– 'No: yesterday he went to wed
One of the brightest wealth has bred.
"It cannot hurt her now," he said,
　　"That I should not be true."'

'Then who is digging on my grave?
　　My nearest dearest kin?'
– 'Ah, no: they sit and think, "What use!
What good will planting flowers produce?
No tendance of her mound can loose
　　Her spirit from Death's gin."'

'But some one digs upon my grave?
　　My enemy? – prodding sly?'
– 'Nay: when she heard you had passed the Gate
That shuts on all flesh soon or late,
She thought you no more worth her hate,
　　And cares not where you lie.'

'Then, who is digging on my grave?
　　Say – since I have not guessed!'
– 'O it is I, my mistress dear,
Your little dog, who still lives near,
And much I hope my movements here
　　Have not disturbed your rest?'

'Ah, yes! *You* dig upon my grave . . .
　　Why flashed it not on me
That one true heart was left behind!
What feeling do we ever find
To equal among human kind
　　A dog's fidelity!'

'Mistress, I dug upon your grave
　　To bury a bone, in case
I should be hungry near this spot
When passing on my daily trot.
I am sorry, but I quite forgot
　　It was your resting-place.'

BIRDS AT WINTER NIGHTFALL

Around the house the flakes fly faster,
And all the berries now are gone
From holly and cotonea-aster
Around the house. The flakes fly! – faster
Shutting indoors that crumb-outcaster
We used to see upon the lawn
Around the house. The flakes fly faster,
And all the berries now are gone!

FAINTHEART IN A RAILWAY TRAIN

At nine in the morning there passed a church,
At ten there passed me by the sea,
At twelve a town of smoke and smirch,
At two a forest of oak and birch,
   And then, on a platform, she:

A radiant stranger, who saw not me.
I said, 'Get out to her do I dare?'
But I kept my seat in my search for a plea,
And the wheels moved on. O could it but be
   That I had alighted there!

THE FROZEN GREENHOUSE

'There was a frost
Last night!' she said,
'And the stove was forgot
When we went to bed,
And the greenhouse plants
Are frozen dead!'

By the breakfast blaze
Blank-faced spoke she,
Her scared young look
Seeming to be
The very symbol
Of tragedy.

47

The frost is fiercer
Than then to-day,
As I pass the place
Of her once dismay,
But the greenhouse stands
Warm, tight, and gay,

While she who grieved
At the sad lot
Of her pretty plants
Cold, iced, forgot –
Herself is colder,
And knows it not.

THE PHOTOGRAPH

The flame crept up the portrait line by line
As it lay on the coals in the silence of night's profound,
  And over the arm's incline,
And along the marge of the silkworm superfine,
And gnawed at the delicate bosom's defenceless round.

Then I vented a cry of hurt, and averted my eyes;
The spectacle was one that I could not bear,
  To my deep and sad surprise;
But, compelled to heed, I again looked furtivewise
Till the flame had eaten her breasts, and mouth, and hair.

'Thank God, she is out of it now!' I said at last,
In a great relief of heart when the thing was done
  That had set my soul aghast,
And nothing was left of the picture unsheathed from the past
But the ashen ghost of the card it had figured on.

She was a woman long hid amid packs of years,
She might have been living or dead; she was lost to my sight,
  And the deed that had nigh drawn tears
Was done in a casual clearance of life's arrears;
But I felt as if I had put her to death that night! . . .

. . . . . .

– Well: she knew nothing thereof did she survive,
And suffered nothing if numbered among the dead;
  Yet – yet – if on earth alive
Did she feel a smart, and with vague strange anguish strive?
If in heaven, did she smile at me sadly and shake her head?

THE VOICE

Woman much missed, how you call to me, call to me,
Saying that now you are not as you were
When you had changed from the one who was all to me,
But as at first, when our day was fair.

Can it be you that I hear? Let me view you, then,
Standing as when I drew near to the town
Where you would wait for me: yes, as I knew you then,
Even to the original air blue gown!

Or is it only the breeze, in its listlessness
Travelling across the wet mead to me here,
You being ever dissolved to wan wistlessness
Heard no more again far or near?

   Thus I; faltering foward,
   Leaves around me falling,
Wind oozing thin through the thorn from norward,
   And the woman calling.

December 1912

THE WOMAN IN THE RYE

'Why do you stand in the dripping rye,
Cold-lipped, unconscious, wet to the knee,
When there are firesides near?' said I.
'I told him I wished him dead,' said she.

'Yea, cried it in my haste to one
Whom I had loved, whom I well loved still;
And die he did. And I hate the sun,
And stand here lonely, aching, chill;

'Stand waiting, waiting under skies
That blow reproach, the while I see
The rooks sheer off to where he lies
Wrapt in a peace withheld from me!'

49

Suggestions for assignments ─────────────

1 How could you tell that all these poems were written by the same person? Write some notes about any similarities of theme, style and language that you find. Use those notes to prepare a poster that shows the similarities. You can use copies of the poems, coloured pens, paste, scissors and anything else that will help.

2 Work in groups and prepare performances of a sequence of some of the poems using appropriate music or pictures. Decide on the best order for the poems you have chosen. You might want to use some of Hardy's poems which you have chosen yourselves from other books. You could include some of your own writing which either puts an alternative view to Hardy's, or is similar in tone and feeling to his.

3 If this was the only evidence you had about Hardy, what would you guess about his life?

   Imagine there is a diary by Hardy. Write the extracts from the diary that relate to the poems here.

7

The Farmer's Bride
Charlotte Mew

THE FARMER'S BRIDE

Three Summers since I chose a maid,
Too young maybe – but more's to do
At harvest-time than bide and woo.
    When us was wed she turned afraid
Of love and me and all things human;
Like the shut of a winter's day.
Her smile went out, and 'twasn't a woman –
    More like a little frightened fay.
        One night, in the Fall, she runned away.

'Out 'mong the sheep, her be,' they said,
'Should properly have been abed;
But sure enough she wasn't there
Lying awake with her wide brown stare.
So over seven-acre field and up-along across the down
    We chased her, flying like a hare
Before our lanterns. To Church-Town
    All in a shiver and a scare
We caught her, fetched her home at last
    And turned the key upon her, fast.

She does the work about the house
As well as most, but like a mouse:
    Happy enough to chat and play
    With birds and rabbits and such as they,
    So long as men-folk keep away.
'Not near, not near!' her eyes beseech
When one of us comes within reach.
    The women say that beasts in stall
    Look round like children at her call.
    I've hardly heard her speak at all.

Shy as a leveret, swift as he,
Straight and slight as a young larch tree,
Sweet as the first wild violets, she,
To her wild self. But what to me?

The short days shorten and the oaks are brown,
  The blue smoke rises to the low grey sky,
One leaf in the still air falls slowly down,
  A magpie's spotted feathers lie
On the black earth spread white with rime,
The berries redden up to Christmas-time.
   What's Christmas-time without there be
   Some other in the house than we!

   She sleeps up in the attic there
   Alone, poor maid. 'Tis but a stair
  Betwixt us. Oh! my God! the down,
  The soft young down of her, the brown,
The brown of her – her eyes, her hair, her hair!

▷   'One night . . . she runned away'

Tell the story of this night from the bride's point of view.

▷ The farmer's way of speaking changes as the poem goes on. Look at the following quotations, and find ways of describing what the differences are.

> Three Summers since I chose a maid
> Too young maybe – but more's to do
> At harvest-time than bide and woo.
>   When us was wed she turned afraid . . .
>
> The short days shorten and the oaks are brown,
>   The blue smoke rises to the low grey sky,
> One leaf in the still air falls slowly down . . .
>
>   . . . Oh! my God! the down,
>   The soft young down of her, the brown,
> The brown of her – her eyes, her hair, her hair!

Why does the way he speaks change like this?

▷

> What's Christmas-time without there be
> Some other in the house than we!
>
> 'Tis but a stair/Betwixt us

At the end of the poem the farmer and his wife are separated by the staircase. Write a piece which expresses the way things are between them. Try it like this:

- Use alternate statements from the farmer and his bride.

- Include unspoken thoughts.

- Tell how each of them feels when alone.

▷ Whose side are you on?

Anthology ───────────────────────────────

UNFAIR TO WOMEN

I thought if only I could marry,
I'd sing and dance and live so gaily;
But all the wedded bliss I see
Is rock the cradle, hush the baby.

Sixteenth-seventeenth century, Welsh: Anon

OVERHEARD IN COUNTY SLIGO

I married a man from County Roscommon
and I live at the back of beyond
with a field of cows and a yard of hens
and six white geese on the pond.

At my door's a square of yellow corn
caught up by its corners and shaken,
and the road runs down through the open gate
and freedom's there for the taking.

I had thought to work on the Abbey stage
or have my name in a book,
to see my thought on the printed page,
or still the crowd with a look.

But I turn to fold the breakfast cloth
and to polish the lustre and brass,
to order and dust the tumbled rooms
and find my face in the glass.

I ought to feel I'm a happy woman
for I lie in the lap of the land,
and I married a man from County Roscommon
and I live in the back of beyond.

Gillian Clarke

NERVOUS PROSTRATION

I married a man of the Croydon class
When I was twenty-two.
And I vex him, and he bores me
Till we don't know what to do!
It isn't good form in the Croydon class
To say you love your wife,
So I spend my days with the tradesmen's books
And pray for the end of life.

In green fields are blossoming trees
And a golden wealth of gorse,
And young birds sing for joy of worms:
It's perfectly clear, of course,
That it wouldn't be taste in the Croydon class
To sing over dinner or tea:
But I sometimes wish the gentleman
Would turn and talk to me!

But every man of the Croydon class
Lives in terror of joy and speech,
'Words are betrayers', 'Joys are brief'
The maxims their wise ones teach.
And for all my labour of love and life
I shall be clothed and fed,
And they'll give me an orderly funeral
When I'm still enough to be dead.

I married a man of the Croydon class
When I was twenty-two.
And I vex him, and he bores me
Till we don't know what to do!
And as I sit in his ordered house,
I feel I must sob or shriek,
To force a man of the Croydon class
To live, or to love, or to speak!

Anna Wickham

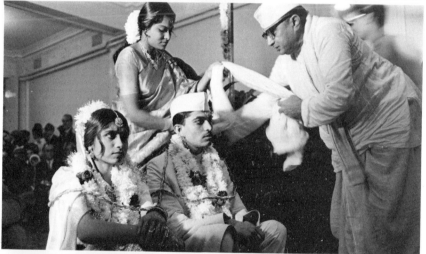

MAJOR MACROO

Major Hawkaby Cole Macroo
Chose
Very wisely
A patient Griselda of a wife with a heart of gold
That never beat for a soul but him
Himself and his slightest whim.

He left her alone for months at a time
When he had to have a change
Just had to
And his pension wouldn't stretch to a fare for two
And he didn't want it to.

And if she wept she was game and nobody knew it
And she stood at the edge of the tunnel and waved as his train went
      through it.

And because it was cheaper they lived abroad
And did he care if she might be unhappy or bored?
He did not.
He'd other things to think of – a lot.

He'd fads and he fed them fat,
And she could lump it and that was that.

He'd several boy friends
And she thought it was nice for him to have them,
And she loved him and felt that he needed her and waited
And waited and never became exasperated.

And when friends came
They went into every room in the house but that one
Which Hawkaby wouldn't have shown.

Such men as these, such selfish cruel men
Hurting what most they love what most loves them,
Never make a mistake when it comes to choosing a woman
To cherish them and be neglected and not think it inhuman.

Stevie Smith

TO MY DEAR AND LOVING
HUSBAND

If ever two were one, then surely we.
If ever man were lov'd by wife, then thee;
If ever wife was happy in a man,
Compare with me ye women if you can.
I prize thy love more than whole Mines of gold,
Or all the riches that the East doth hold.
My love is such that Rivers cannot quench,
Nor ought but love from thee give recompence.
Thy love is such I can no way repay,
The heavens reward thee manifold I pray.
Then while we live, in love lets so persever,
That when we live no more, we may live ever.

Anna Bradstreet

Suggestions for assignments ⸺⸺⸺⸺⸺

1 Write a piece about the poems in this anthology which looks at the men's point of view. Try one of these forms:

- a letter from the man in one of the poems to a male friend

- a monologue by the man

- an interview with one or more of the husbands after the loss of their wives

- a poem in which the man speaks and tells his story

Share your piece with other people, and talk about what emerges.

2 Make your own anthology, beginning with these poems and adding your own writing. You could include things other people tell you about marriage and relationships, song titles and lyrics, photographs with captions.

8

Half-caste
John Agard

I n the book *The Heart of the Race*, a woman describes being at a
conference where there was a discussion of mixed race. She says:

> A lot of women there were angry about terms like 'half-caste' and
> 'coloured' because they saw them as being divisive. When you
> think about it, even the word sounds like a put down, like
> 'half-done' ... As far as I'm concerned, I'm a *Black* woman,
> because I live that reality.
>
> (*The Heart of the Race* by Beverley Bryan)

John Agard, originally from Guyana, describes himself as

> Me not no Oxford don,
> me a simple immigrant
> from Clapham Common
> I didn't graduate
> I immigrate

In the next poem, John Agard writes about 'half-caste' in ways that
force readers to ask what the phrase actually means.

HALF-CASTE

Excuse me
standing on one leg
I'm half-caste

Explain yuself
wha yu mean
when yu say half-caste
yu mean when picasso
mix red an green
is a half-caste canvas/
explain yuself
wha yu mean
when yu say half-caste
yu mean when light an shadow
mix in de sky
is a half-caste weather/
well in dat case
england weather
nearly always half-caste
in fact some o dem cloud
half-caste till dem overcast
so spiteful dem dont want de sun pass
ah rass/
explain yuself
wha yu mean
when you say half-caste
yu mean tchaikovsky
sit down at dah piano
an mix a black key
wid a white key
is a half-caste symphony/

Explain yuself
wha yu mean
Ah listening to yu wid de keen
half of mih ear
Ah lookin at yu wid de keen
half a mih eye
an when I'm introduced to yu
I'm sure you'll understand
why I offer yu half-a-hand
an when I sleep at night
I close half-a-eye
consequently when I dream
I dream half-a-dream
an when moon begin to glow
I half-caste human being
cast half-a-shadow
but yu must come back tomorrow

wid de whole of yu eye
an de whole of yu ear
an de whole of yu mind

an I will tell yu
de other half
of my story

▷ Read the poem aloud. Work in pairs and try it in different ways:

- as though you are angry with another person
- as though you are having a polite conversation
- as though you are having a debate
- as though you are trying to understand what another person feels
- as though you are making fun of the person who is using the words

Did one of these readings feel easier to do?

▷ Work in pairs and study the language in which this poem has been deliberately written, looking especially at these things:

- forms of Standard English used (e.g. 'Excuse me')

- non-standard spelling (e.g. 'yu, yuself')

- non-standard grammar (e.g. 'england weather')

- punctuation

- repetition of words, structures and other patterns (e.g. 'Explain yuself...')

List examples under those headings, and make notes of anything else you notice.
What kind of English is the poem written in?
Why did John Agard choose to write it the way he did?

▷ Here are the final seven lines of the poem rewritten in Standard English:

> but you must come back tomorrow
>
> with the whole of your eye
> and the whole of your ear
> and the whole of your mind
>
> and I will tell you
> the other half
> of my story

What difference does it make if the poem is written like this?

▷ People may have very different feelings about the word 'half-caste'. List arguments explaining why it is or is not a good title for the poem.
Working in pairs, construct an argument, with one person saying 'half-caste' is a bad title and another saying it is a good title. You can either do this orally, or in a piece of writing.

Anthology _____

In this poem, a man knows that he is hiding his real self from the world.
The writer was a white New Zealander.

AS OTHERS SEE US

With 'No Admittance' printed on my heart,
    I go abroad, and play my public part;
And win applause – I have no cause to be
    Ashamed of that strange self that others see.

But how can I reveal to you, and you,
    My real self's hidden and unlovely hue?
How can I undeceive, how end despair
    Of this intolerable make-believe?

You must see with God's eyes, or I must wear
    My furtive failures stark upon my sleeve.

Basil Dowling

The next poem was written at the time when Britain was involved in the
slave trade.

PITY FOR POOR AFRICANS

Video meliora proboque,
Deteriora sequor.*

I own I am shock'd at the purchase of slaves,
And fear those who buy them and sell them are knaves;
What I hear of their hardships, their tortures, and groans,
Is almost enough to draw pity from stones.

I pity them greatly, but I must be mum,
For how could we do without sugar and rum?
Especially sugar, so needful we see;
What, give up our desserts, our coffee, and tea!

Besides if we do, the French, Dutch, and Danes
Will heartily thank us, no doubt, for our pains;
If we do not buy the poor creatures, they will;
And tortures and groans will be multiplied still.

If foreigners likewise would give up the trade,
Much more in behalf of your wish might be said;
But, while they get riches by purchasing blacks,
Pray tell me why we may not also go snacks?

Your scruples and arguments bring to my mind
A story so pat, you may think it is coin'd,
On purpose to answer you, out of my mint;
But I can assure you I saw it in print.

A youngster at school, more sedate than the rest,
Had once his integrity put to the test;
His comrades had plotted an orchard to rob,
And ask'd him to go and assist in the job.

He was shock'd, sir, like you, and answer'd, 'Oh no!
What! rob our good neighbour? I pray you don't go!
Besides, the man's poor, his orchard's his bread:
Then think of his children, for they must be fed.'

'You speak very fine, and you look very grave,
But apples we want, and apples we'll have;
If you will go with us, you shall have a share,
If not, you shall have neither apple nor pear.'

They spoke, and Tom ponder'd – 'I see they will go;
Poor man! what a pity to injure him so!
Poor man! I would save him his fruit if I could,
But staying behind will do him no good.

'If the matter depended alone upon me,
His apples might hang till they dropp'd from the tree;
But since they will take them, I think I'll go too;
He will lose none by me, though I get a few.'

His scruples thus silenced, Tom felt more at ease,
And went with his comrades the apples to seize;
He blamed and protested, but join'd in the plan;
He shared in the plunder, but pitied the man.

William Cowper

* I see the best, but follow the worst.

The author of the following poem is a Black South African.

MY NAME

Nomgqibelo Ncamisile Mnqhibisa

Look what they have done to my name . . .
the wonderful name of my great-great-grandmothers
Nomgqibelo Ncamisile Mnqhibisa

The burly bureaucrat was surprised.
What he heard was music to his ears
'Wat is daai, sê nou weer?'
'I am from Chief Daluxolo Velayigodle of emaMpodweni
And my name is *Nomgqibelo Ncamisile Mnqhibisa*.'

Messia, help me!
My name is so simple
and yet so meaningful,
but to this man it is trash . . .

He gives me a name
Convenient enough to answer his whim:
I end up being
Maria . . .
I . . .
Nomgqibelo Ncamisile Mnqhibisa.

Magoleng wa Selepe

The writer of this piece was born in Glasgow.

FOREIGN

Imagine living in a strange, dark city for twenty years.
There are some dismal dwellings on the east side
and one of them is yours. On the landing, you hear
your foreign accent echo down the stairs. You think
in a language of your own and talk in theirs.

Then you are writing home. The voice in your head
recites the letter in a local dialect; behind that
is the sound of your mother singing to you,
all that time ago, and now you do not know
why your eyes are watering and what's the word for this.

You use the public transport. Work. Sleep. Imagine one night
you saw a name for yourself sprayed in red
against a brick wall. A hate name. Red like blood.
It is snowing on the streets, under the neon lights,
as if this place were coming to bits before your eyes.

And in the delicatessen, from to time, the coins
in your palm will not translate. Inarticulate,
because this is not home, you point at fruit. Imagine
that one of you says *Me not know what these people mean.
It like they only go to bed and dream.* Imagine that.

Carol Ann Duffy

Grace Nichols was born in Guyana and came to the UK in 1977.

EPILOGUE

I have crossed an ocean
I have lost my tongue
from the root of the old one
a new one has sprung

Grace Nichols

Suggestions for assignments _____

1 Write something of your own to go with the poems in this anthology. Decide where you want to place your writing in the sequence, and whether it will be one long piece or several shorter pieces.

2 You have already done some work on the language of the John Agard poem, which you could now write up.

Look at the language of the other poems in the way you studied the language of John Agard's poem. Some questions you could ask yourself are:

- Why does Grace Nichols write in Standard English?

- How would you describe William Cowper's English?

- Why are there different languages in Selepe's poem?

3 The issues raised in this unit are about people's freedom to be themselves. Write an essay about this question:

How does language help or prevent people being themselves?

Look at the way the different poems presented here give different answers to that question. Also include your own experiences and those of your friends.

9

House-Talk
Fleur Adcock

▷ The poem is called 'House-Talk'. How many different meanings can you find for the title?

▷ The poem is about a mother who is lying in bed. The house she lives in is old, and she can hear her son and his friends, who have just come in late.

Work with others and make a list of all the things that a mother might feel at a time like this.

The first two verses of the poem follow:

Through my pillow, through mattress, carpet, floor and ceiling,
sounds ooze up from the room below:
footsteps, chinking crockery, hot-water pipes groaning,
the muffled clunk of the refrigerator door,
and voices. They are trying to be quiet,
my son and his friends, home late in the evening.

Tones come softly filtered through the layers of the padding.
I hear the words but not what the words are,
as on my radio when the batteries are fading.
Voices are reduced to a muted music:
Andrew's bass, his friend's tenor, the indistinguishable
light murmurs of the girls; occasional giggling.

Did you list any feelings that don't match what this mother feels?

▷ Discuss in your group which of the sentences below best describe how she feels. You can choose more than one, or you can write your own, if you think these aren't right.

- She feels it's a familiar, comforting experience.

- She wants to hear what they're saying.

- She's pleased she's no longer alone in the house.

- She enjoys hearing the other sounds.

- She's worried about what they're doing.

- She feels affection for them.

- She can relax now and go to sleep.

▷ There's another verse to this poem. After your discussion of how the mother feels, what would you think should be in it? Write a short paragraph predicting what the verse will be about, and compare it with what other people have written.

Here is the last verse.

> Surely wood and plaster retain something
> in their grain of all the essences they absorb?
> This house has been lived in for ninety years,
> nine by us. It has heard all manner of talking.
> Its porous fabric must be saturated
> with words. I offer it my peaceful breathing.

Is this what you expected?

▷ Compare this with the suggestions you made at the beginning about the title. Which of the meanings best fits the poem now?

HOUSE-TALK

Through my pillow, through mattress, carpet, floor and ceiling,
sounds ooze up from the room below:
footsteps, chinking crockery, hot-water pipes groaning,
the muffled clunk of the refrigerator door,
and voices. They are trying to be quiet,
my son and his friends, home late in the evening.

Tones come softly filtered through the layers of the padding.
I hear the words but not what the words are,
as on my radio when the batteries are fading.
Voices are reduced to a muted music:
Andrew's bass, his friend's tenor, the indistinguishable
light murmurs of the girls; occasional giggling.

Surely wood and plaster retain something
in their grain of all the essences they absorb?
This house has been lived in for ninety years,
nine by us. It has heard all manner of talking.
Its porous fabric must be saturated
with words. I offer it my peaceful breathing.

▷ Some words and phrases in the poem can be listed under the heading
of 'house':
　　for example, 'carpet, floor and ceiling'

Some can go under 'talk':
　　for example, 'voices', 'all manner of talking'

Some can go under 'noises':
　　for example, 'chinking', 'muted music'

Make lists of words from the poem under those three headings. Talk
about the patterns that appear, both under each heading and
between the lists.

Look at the words 'ooze', 'filtered', 'absorb', 'porous' and
'saturated'.

What have they got in common? How do they apply to the idea of
sounds in a house?

Anthology ─────────────────────────────

SHADOWS OF MY MOTHER
AGAINST A WALL

The wood-pigeon rolls soft notes off its breast
in a tree which grows by a fence.
The smell of creosote,
easy as wild gum
oozing from tree boles
keeps me awake. A thunderstorm
heckles the air.

I step into a bedroom
pungent with child's sleep,
and lift the potty and pile of picture books
so my large shadow
crosses his eyes.

Sometimes at night, expectant,
I think I see the shadow of my mother
bridge a small house of enormous rooms.
Here are white, palpable walls
and stories of my grandmother:
the old hours of tenderness I missed.

Helen Dunmore

A FAMILY MAN

At night when the ordinary loves have settled
like dust drifting a little in my son's cough, my wife's breath, my
    daughter's sigh,
I call them in. From the dark side of leaves,
from the countries of desire, from the cracks in the road,
from the places I went to and never gave back
at the border, the faces I wanted and never forgave
For dying, from the dark side of leaves, they come
Softer than smoke, shadows on paper,
The dust drifting a little in my wife's cough, my son's sigh, my
    daughter's breath.
They make hoarse journeys in my head. They cry
at the lamp's white pain. I silence them.
They orbit, tongueless. They die like stars; they cool
to ash. I trace their stain on paper, and sign it. Watch them
wind my life down like small, burnt moons. Watch them fall
like dust drifting a little in my daughter's cough, my wife's sigh,
    my son's breath.

Dennis Scott

Suggestions for assignments

1 Write about lying in bed, not quite asleep, with all the familiar
sounds and shapes around you, and the mind ranging freely and easily
over thoughts and memories. Use these notes to help you:

- Are you writing as yourself or as an invented character?
- What other people are in the house?
- What sounds can you hear, both inside and outside the room?
- What memories come back to you, about your life, the house, other
  places you've lived in or visited?

As you think about these questions, consider the beginnings of the
poems in this unit, their titles and how they use details.

2 Work in a group to talk about the poems in the unit. Use those
questions to guide your conversation.

- What can the three poets hear?
- What are they thinking of as they lie awake?
- Identify unexpected or difficult words or phrases in the three poems,
  and produce explanations of their meaning which satisfy you and
  your group.
- Describe how each poet feels at the end of his or her poem.

10

I heard a fly buzz...
Emily Dickinson

I heard a fly buzz when I died;
The stillness in the room
Was like the stillness in the air
Between the heaves of storm.

The eyes around had wrung them dry,
And breaths were gathering firm
For that last onset when the King
Be witnessed in the room.

I willed my keepsakes, signed away
What portion of me be
Assignable – and then it was
There interposed a fly,

With blue, uncertain, stumbling buzz,
Between the light and me;
And then the windows failed, and then
I could not see to see.

This is a photograph taken in 1855. It is called *Fading Away*.

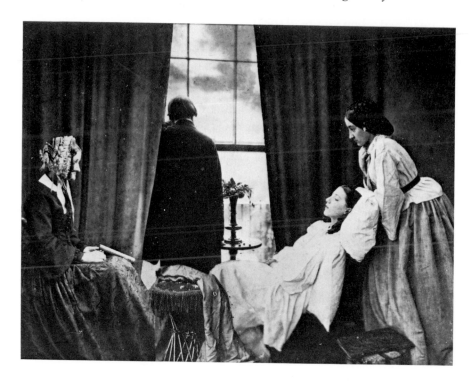

▷ Do you think the photograph matches the poem?
Does the person dying in the photograph look like the person you imagined when you read the poem?

▷ Normally when we read something with an 'I' in it, we assume the writer is writing about something that happened to him or her.
What is the effect of using 'I' in this poem?

▷ Here are 24 words, describing different feelings which the dying person in the poem might be having before and after the fly 'interposes'.
Choose five of them which seem to you to be closest to what the person in the poem was feeling.

CONFIDENT	IRRITATED	TRIUMPHANT	NUMB
HAPPY	RELAXED	COMPOSED	DESPAIRING
HOPEFUL	EXASPERATED	PANICKY	RESIGNED
UNCERTAIN	ANXIOUS	AMUSED	SURPRISED
SATISFIED	SAD	EXCITED	PROUD
DISAPPOINTED	RELIEVED	COMFORTED	PREPARED

When you've chosen the five words, write five statements using each word in this frame:

She is _ _ _ _ _ _ _ _ _ _ because _ _ _ _ _ _ _ _ _ _ _

Do your five words have anything in common?

This is the way Emily Dickinson actually set out the poem. How is it different from the version printed on page 76?

> I heard a Fly buzz – when I died –
> The Stillness in the Room
> Was like the Stillness in the Air –
> Between the Heaves of Storm –
>
> The Eyes around – had wrung them dry –
> And Breaths were gathering firm
> For that last Onset – when the King
> Be witnessed – in the Room
>
> I willed my Keepsakes – Signed away
> What portion of me be
> Assignable – and then it was
> There interposed a Fly –
>
> With Blue – uncertain stumbling Buzz –
> Between the light – and me –
> And then the Windows failed – and then
> I could not see to see –

Does it make a difference to the way you read it to have the poem set out like this?

DEATH

When my eyes are fogged
And my ears are clogged
And my nose turns cold
And my tongue's back rolled
And my cheeks slacken
And my lips blacken
And my mouth blubbers
And my spittle slobbers
And my hair stands up
And my heart-beats droop
And my hands quiver
And my feet stiffen, –
All too late, all too late,
When the bier is at the gate!

> Then I shall go
> From bed to floor,
> From floor to shroud,
> From shroud to bier,
> From bier to pit
> And be shut in it.

Then lies my house upon my nose,
And all my care for this world goes.

Medieval: Anon

FROM 'OF THE LAST VERSES IN THE BOOK'

The Soul's dark cottage, batter'd and decay'd
Lets in new light through chinks that time has made;
Stronger by weakness, wiser men become,
As they draw near to their eternal home:
Leaving the Old, both worlds at once they view,
That stand upon the threshold of the New.

Edmund Waller

ALL SOUL'S DAY

Be careful, then, and be gentle about death.
For it is hard to die, it is difficult to go through
the door, even when it opens.

And the poor dead, when they have left the walled
and silvery city of the now hopeless body
where are they to go, Oh, where are they to go?

They linger in the shadow of the earth.
The earth's long conical shadow is full of souls
that cannot find the way across the sea of change.

Be kind, Oh be kind to your dead
and give them a little encouragement
and help them to build their little ship of death

For the soul has a long, long journey after death
to the sweet home of pure oblivion.
Each needs a little ship, a little ship
and the proper store of meal for the longest journey.

Oh, from out of your heart
provide for your dead once more, equip them
like departing mariners, lovingly.

D H Lawrence

Normal family life carried on: his mother sat beside him, the children went to school, the sun shone. June, the district nurse, was briskly down to earth. 'If he dies in the night,' she warned me, 'don't call the doctor until morning, because he won't come!' And although we had accepted for months that Andy was dying, she told me firmly, 'You must let him go.' She was right. I stopped trying to involve Andy in the life that was leaving him behind and concentrated instead on letting him move towards death.

Late one night, Andy's breathing became laboured. The locum GP said, 'You do know he is very, very ill?' meaning, 'You do realise this man is dying?' I assured him I knew. Somehow I also knew this night would be our last together. I held Andy in my arms and talked to him for hours. I told him that he was dying, that he need not worry about me, our children or his elderly mother. He had fought long enough: it was time for us both to let go.

He took three last breaths and at 4.43 am time stopped for him. Although he lay still and sightless, I knew the essence of him was there with me and I kept right on talking while I closed his eyes, washed his face and called the children in.

The hours after his death were totally private. We could each say goodbye in our own time, our own way. There was no one to pull curtains around his bed, send his body to the mortuary or hand me a bundle of his clothes. We all look back on Andy's final illness as a positive time of immense tenderness which we were privileged to share. Perhaps it was Andy's last gift. With his passing went all our fear of death.

Claudia Melnyk

Suggestions for assignments _____

1 Work in pairs or small groups. Read the pieces in the anthology together and talk about them. Some of the questions that are raised by the pieces are:

- Is death the final end?

- What can the living do to help the dying?

- Should the dying be allowed to choose whether to die at home or in hospital?

- How do people usually talk about death?

Write your own reflections. You can include:

– things that were said in your discussion
– things that occur to you now that you are writing

2 What can you learn from the pieces in this unit about what these people think and feel about dying?

11

Mariana
Alfred, Lord Tennyson

MARIANA

'Mariana in the moated grange.' – *Measure for Measure*

With blackest moss the flower-plots
   Were thickly crusted, one and all:
The rusted nails fell from the knots
   That held the peach to the garden-wall.
The broken sheds looked sad and strange:
   Unlifted was the clinking latch;
   Weeded and worn the ancient thatch
Upon the lonely moated grange.
     She only said, 'My life is dreary,
       He cometh not,' she said;
     She said, 'I am aweary, aweary.
       I would that I were dead!'

Her tears fell with the dews at even;
   Her tears fell ere the dews were dried;
She could not look on the sweet heaven,
   Either at morn or eventide.
After the flitting of the bats,
   When thickest dark did trance the sky,
   She drew her casement-curtain by,
And glanced athwart the glooming flats.
     She only said, 'The night is dreary,
       He cometh not,' she said;
     She said, 'I am aweary, aweary,
       I would that I were dead!'

Upon the middle of the night,
   Waking she heard the night-fowl crow:
The cock sung out an hour ere light:
   From the dark fen the oxen's low
Came to her: without hope of change,
   In sleep she seemed to walk forlorn,
   Till cold winds woke the grey-eyed morn
About the lonely moated grange.
     She only said, 'The day is dreary,
       He cometh not,' she said;
     She said, 'I am aweary, aweary,
       I would that I were dead!'

About a stone-cast from the wall
   A sluice with blackened waters slept,
And o'er it many, round and small,
   The clustered marish-mosses crept.
Hard by a poplar shook alway,
   All silver-green with gnarlèd bark:
   For leagues no other tree did mark
The level waste, the rounding gray.
     She only said, 'My life is dreary,
      He cometh not,' she said;
     She said, 'I am aweary, aweary,
      I would that I were dead!'

And ever when the moon was low,
   And the shrill winds were up and away,
In the white curtain, to and fro,
   She saw the gusty shadow sway.
But when the moon was very low,
   And wild winds bound within their cell,
   The shadow of the poplar fell
Upon her bed, across her brow.
     She only said, 'The night is dreary,
      He cometh not,' she said;
     She said, 'I am aweary, aweary,
      I would that I were dead!'

All day within the dreamy house,
   The doors upon their hinges creaked;
The blue fly sung in the pane: the mouse
   Behind the mouldering wainscot shrieked,
Or from the crevice peered about.
   Old faces glimmered thro' the doors,
   Old footsteps trod the upper floors,
Old voices called her from without.
     She only said, 'My life is dreary,
      He cometh not,' she said;
     She said, 'I am aweary, aweary,
      I would that I were dead!'

▷ As part of becoming familiar with this poem, try different ways of reading it aloud – for instance, working in threes and sharing out the poem between you in various ways.

Tennyson was prompted to write this poem by a reference in Shakespeare's play to a woman who was jilted and abandoned by a callous lover.

▷ Write a version of 'Mariana' in poetry or narrative, set in a modern environment. Work in pairs through each of the following stages.

Step One
List the details in the poem, about

• the general landscape

• the immediate surroundings of the building

• the interior of the building

Step Two
Begin your version with a description of the place you have chosen. It should create the same sense of being cut off from the world, and the same atmosphere, as 'Mariana'. Note the way the poem uses the details you collected in your list.

Step Three
Make lists of colours, sounds, movements and light in 'Mariana'. Find similar details for your description.

Step Four
Reread the parts of the poem about the poplar tree. Decide why it is significant, and what its equivalent in your piece will be.

Step Five
Will your Mariana behave in the same way? What will she do, and what will she say? (What do you think of the way Mariana behaves in the poem?)

Prepare your version as a presentation for others in the group.

Anthology ───────────────────────

I DO NOT WANT TO BE
YOUR WEEPING WOMAN

I do not want to be your weeping woman
holding you to me with a chain of grief.

I could more easily bear the flame of your anger
than the frost of your kisses empty of desire:

I do not want to be your gentle lover
dragging you to me on a rope of pity.

Sooner that you never touched me than that you ever
should touch me from a distance made of mercy:

I do not want to be your silent mother
always forgiving and smiling and never loving.

If you forget me, forget me utterly. Never
come to my arms without interest. I shall know it:

I do not want to be your weeping woman
pinning you to me with a sword of tears.

I do not want to be your weeping woman.

Alison Boodson

NARRATIVE

Translated from the Afrikaans by the poet

A woman grew, with waiting, over-quiet.
The earth along its spiralled path was spun
through many a day and night, now green, now dun;
at times she laughed, and then, at times, she cried.

The years went by. By turns she woke and slept
through the long hours of night, but every day
she went, as women go, her casual way,
and no one knew what patient tryst she kept.

Hope and despair tread their alternate round
and merge into acceptance, till at length
the years have only quietness in store.

And so at last the narrative has found
in her its happy end: this tranquil strength
is better than the thing she's waiting for.

Elizabeth Eybers

RESURRECTION

My candle burns up lank and fair,
The gale is on the pane,
The dead leaves on the whirlwind's branch
Are risen trees again.

And can I sleep tonight, my heart,
With candle and with storm?
And dare I sleep, my heart, my heart,
And see my dreams alone?

For when in my resurgent hands
I take the mirror weedy with brown hair:
Rustling the dark wind through the glass –
Oh, who is there?

Margiad Evans

A MISSING PERSON

In the darkened room
a woman
cannot find her reflection in the mirror

waiting as usual
at the edge of sleep.

In her hands she holds
the oil lamp
whose drunken yellow flames
know where her lonely body hides.

Jayanta Mahapatra

Suggestions for assignments ⸻

1 Construct a collage which includes all the poems in this unit (either using them whole or choosing lines from them) and pictures you have collected from magazines, newspapers, photograph collections and any other suitable source. You may decide to add your own words and pictures you have drawn or painted yourselves. Give your collage a title.

If you prefer, you could work on your own with one of the poems in the anthology. Produce a picture which illustrates the poem, as 'Mariana' was illustrated by the painting 'Mariana in the Moated Grange'.

2 Each poem presents a different image of a woman. Make a list for each poem of the characteristics of the woman in that poem and then add your own feelings and opinions about the woman.

One way of doing this would be to work as a group with a large piece of paper. Draw five boxes, one each for Mariana and the four poems in the anthology. In each box, compile your individual lists for that poem. You can write comments in the spaces between to show the links.

How lifelike and accurate do you think these images of women are?

12

Men Talk

When Bob was young, He told everyone He was going to grow up to be a cartoon and they all laughed at him. But no one is laughing now.

hickerson

THE POINT OF VIEW.

Exasperated Old Gentleman (to Lady in front of him). "Excuse me, Madam, but my Seat has cost me Ten Shillings, and I want to see. Your Hat—"
The Lady. "My Hat has cost me Ten Guineas, Sir, and I want it to be seen!"

SNOOPY © 1958

Humour is very personal: what makes you laugh may not amuse your friends, and sometimes other people's sense of humour may seem very odd to you.

Read the poems in this unit, to yourself first. Which of them appeal to your sense of humour?

Does it make a difference when you read them aloud or share them in a group?

MEN TALK

Women
Rabbit rabbit rabbit women
Tattle and titter
Women prattle
Women waffle and witter

Men Talk. Men Talk.

Women into Girl Talk
About Women's Trouble
Trivia 'n' Small Talk
They yap and they babble

Men Talk. Men Talk.

Women yatter
Women chatter
Women chew the fat, women spill the beans
Women aint been takin'
The oh-so Good Advice in them
Women's Magazines.

A Man Likes A Good Listener.

Oh yeah
I like A Woman
Who likes me enough
Not to nitpick
Not to nag and
Not to interrupt 'cause I call that treason
A woman with the Good Grace
To be struck dumb
By me Sweet Reason. Yes –

A Man Likes a Good Listener

A Real
Man
Likes a Real Good Listener

women yap yap yap
Verbal Diarrhoea is a Female Disease
Woman she spread she rumours round she
Like Philadelphia Cream Cheese.

Oh
Bossy Women Gossip

Girlish Women Giggle
Women natter, women nag
Women niggle niggle niggle

Men Talk.

Men
Think First. Speak Later
Men Talk

Liz Lochhead

THE COMPUTER'S FIRST PROVERBS
After Edwin Morgan

You can take a dog to the keyside, but you can't push him in
all is wet that starts to bark
if you pay peanuts you get them planted in the park
nothing should be done in haste but grip your trout
if you want fish, you must prepare for stink
he who fishes with the piper barks like a dog
he who fishes a tiger is afraid to wink
fish will out, fish will out
all roaring is the same in the dark.

A dog in the brook is worth avoiding
think of a fountain and you froth in the head
speech is water, fish are water
it is too late to rub in embrocation after the dream has gone
strike while the law is out
put the stout dog to a deaf oven
flush the fridge if you have a long arm
idle lips make the best smoke rings
fishmongers always make room
it is all melted than ends melted
in May let the plugs bloom
You cannot roar with the workers and ignore the phone
it takes three waders to make a wet man
the longest dog winks all the way home

An Improvisation on the Oxford Dictionary of Proverbs

Peter Finch

SHO NUFF

Cold soft drinks
quenched my thirst
one hot and humid July day
after a cool drive
to a mountain store.
Seems like every woman
in the place
had on halter tops
displaying their expensive tans.
There were two women
standing in front of me
at the checkout counter.
One said to the other,
'You must be a lady of leisure,
just look at your beautiful tan.'
Then the other woman responded,
'No, you must be a lady of leisure,
yours is much darker than mine.'
A tall dark and handsome Black dude
standing behind me
whispering down my Black back
s
    a
      i
        d
'Sister, if those two
are ladies of leisure,
you must surely be
a lady of royalty.'
And in a modest tone, I replied,
'SHO NUFF?'

Nilene O A Foxworth

THE TRADITIONAL
GRAMMARIAN AS POET

Haiku, you ku, he,
She, or it kus, we ku, you
Ku, they ku. Thang ku.

Ted Hipple

95

THE SNIFFLE

In spite of her sniffle
Isabel's chiffle.
Some girls with a sniffle
Would be weepy and tiffle;
They would look awful,
Like a rained-on waffle,
But Isabel's chiffle
In spite of her sniffle.
Her nose is more red
With a cold in her head,
But then, to be sure,
Her eyes are bluer.
Some girls with a snuffle,
Their tempers are uffle.
But when Isabel's snivelly
She's snivelly civilly,
And when she's snuffly
She's perfectly luffly.

Ogden Nash

THE CHEETAH, MY DEAREST,
IS KNOWN NOT TO CHEAT

The cheetah, my dearest, is known not to cheat;
the tiger possesses no tie;
the horse-fly, of course, was never a horse;
the lion will not tell a lie.

The turkey, though perky, was never a Turk;
nor the monkey ever a monk;
the mandrel, though like one, was never a man,
but some men are like him, when drunk.

The springbok, dear thing, was not born in the Spring;
the walrus will not build a wall.
No badger is bad; no adder can add.
There is no truth in these things at all.

George Barker

96

WHA FE CALL I'

Miss Ivy, tell me supmn,
An mi wan' yuh ansa good.
When yuh eat roun 12 o'clock,
Wassit yuh call yuh food?

For fram mi come yah mi confuse,
An mi noh know which is right,
Weddah dinnah a de food yuh eat midday,
Or de one yuh eat a night.

Mi know sey breakfus a de mawnin one
But cyan tell ef suppa a six or t'ree,
An one ting mi wi nebba undastan,
Is when yuh hab yuh tea.

Miss A dung a London ha lunch 12 o'clock,
An dinnah she hab bout t'ree,
Suppa she hab bout six o'clock,
But she noh hab noh tea.

Den mi go a Cambridge todda day,
Wi hab dinnah roun' bout two,
T'ree hour later mi frien she sey,
Mi hungry, how bout yuh?

Joe sey im tink a suppa time,
An mi sey yes, mi agree,
She halla, 'Suppa? a five o'clock,
Missis yuh mussa mean tea!'

Den Sunday mi employer get up late,
Soh she noh hab breakfus nor lunch,
But mi hear she a talk bout 'Elevenses',
An one sinting dem call 'Brunch'.

Breakfus, elevenses, an brunch,
lunch, dinnah, suppa, tea,
Mi brain cyan wuk out which is which,
An when a de time fe hab i'.

For jus' when mi mek headway,
Sinting dreadful set mi back,
An dis when mi tink mi know dem all,
Mi hear bout one name snack.

Mi noh tink mi a badda wid no name,
Mi dis a nyam when time mi hungry,
For doah mi 'tomach wi glad fe de food,
I' couldn care less whey mi call i'.

Valerie Bloom

Suggestions for assignments _____

Men Talk
Whose voice is speaking in the poem – a man's or a woman's? You
could write your own commentary on the differences between men and
women – dress sense? dancing styles? work? friendships? Write using a
man's voice, or a woman's voice, or both in turn. Notice that this poem,
which appears to be critical of women, is written by a woman.

The Computer's First Proverbs
The writer based this on Edwin Morgan's idea of a computer trying to
write a Christmas card, and drawing on its bank of ready-made,
appropriate, but misused, words and phrases. He has also used a source
book. See what your 'computer' comes up with – the computer's first
top twenty? the computer's Valentine, or Mother's Day card? Or try a
different book like the *Guinness Book of Records*.

Sho Nuff
What's the point of this poem?

The Traditional Grammarian As Poet
How would you explain this little poem to someone who didn't know
what a haiku was? And while you're about it, see if you can explain the
title as well.

The Sniffle
Odgen Nash often played around with rhyme, taking it to its logical but
bizarre conclusion, as he does here. See if you can find any other poems
by Nash; and can you work as a group and produce your own crazy but
accurate rhymes?

The Cheetah
The poem plays with names and takes part of them completely literally.
Try this yourself with something of your own choice: favourite or
disliked bands and groups? names of towns? clothes? names of cars?
names of people – in your class, for instance?

Wha Fe Call I'
Are there other things that it's easy to get confused about, like
'tea/supper, lunch/dinner'? How important is it? Notice the last verse of
Valerie Bloom's poem. Try writing a reply to Valerie Bloom in Standard
English, maybe as a series of telephone calls from different people,
explaining what the differences are between lunch, dinner, tea, supper
and so on.

General assignments

1 A spellchecker on a word processor can produce some amazing
alternatives, especially to people's names, which can enliven even dull
poems; and so can using a global replace. If you have access to a word
processor, see what it can do. Try the names of politicians, or famous
people in the news.

2 Work as a group and make your own collection of poems you all find
funny, or at least amusing. Present your collection, either on tape or in
performance.

13

Miracle on St David's Day
Gillian Clarke

MIRACLE ON ST DAVID'S DAY

'They flash upon that inward eye
Which is the bliss of solitude'
'The Daffodils' by W. Wordsworth

An afternoon yellow and open-mouthed
with daffodils. The sun treads the path
among cedars and enormous oaks.
It might be a country house, guests strolling,
the rumps of gardeners between nursery shrubs.

I am reading poetry to the insane.
An old woman, interrupting, offers
as many buckets of coal as I need.
A beautiful chestnut-haired boy listens
entirely absorbed. A schizophrenic

on a good day, they tell me later.
In a cage of first March sun a woman
sits not listening, not seeing, not feeling.
In her neat clothes the woman is absent.
A big, mild man is tenderly led

to his chair. He has never spoken.
His labourer's hands on his knees, he rocks
gently to the rhythms of the poems.
I read to their presences, absences,
to the big, dumb labouring man as he rocks.

He is suddenly standing, silently,
huge and mild, but I feel afraid. Like slow
movement of spring water or the first bird
of the year in the breaking darkness,
the labourer's voice recites 'The Daffodils'.

The nurses are frozen, alert; the patients
seem to listen. He is hoarse but word-perfect.
Outside the daffodils are still as wax,
a thousand, ten thousand, their syllables
unspoken, their creams and yellows still.

Forty years ago, in a Valleys school,
the class recited poetry by rote.
Since the dumbness of misery fell
he has remembered there was a music
of speech and that once he had something to say.

When he's done, before the applause, we observe
the flowers' silence. A thrush sings
and the daffodils are flame.

This poem tells a story. There are things the poet doesn't tell us in the poem:

- whether she's been here before
- why she's doing this
- what the inside of the mental hospital looked like to her
- how she felt when she saw the patients
- what she saw when she looked around her
- what she thought when the old woman interrupted her
- how she felt about the audience as she was reading
- why she felt afraid when the man stood up
- what she did while the man was reciting
- what happened afterwards
- what she and the nurses talked about after the reading was finished
- what difference the whole experience has made to her

▷ Write a story called 'Miracle on St David's Day', using the poem, and adding to it your solutions to the problems above.

▷ Did the daffodils play an important part in your story? How do they matter in the poem?

It's a true story, and I told it many times before I found a way to write the poem. The occupational therapist of a mental hospital invited me to read poems to the patients on the first of March, St David's Day. It was a beautiful spring afternoon, and daffodils lit the lawns about the occupational therapy centre, which stood among trees apart from the main building.

There were about fifteen patients present. Some listened alertly, others were so blank and still that I could sense the silence behind their eyes, and a few interrupted me, thinking they were somewhere else.

Walter, the dumb man, was a Council workman suffering from a depression so profound that he had lost the power of speech, though there was nothing physically wrong with him. Long ago, when he was a child in one of the coal-mining valleys of South Wales, where education was very highly regarded, he and his class-mates had learned poems by heart, as they had learned their tables and many other things. He was suddenly reminded of Wordsworth's poem, and his silence was unlocked.

The poem is about the power of language, especially poetry. Our minds are full of voices, and our bodies – tongues, ears, hands, feet – love sound and rhythm. Poetry is easier to memorise than prose, and its works of art are free and can be carried anywhere and turned to in the loneliest moments – in hospital, in prison, in exile.

At first I tried to write a poem about voices speaking out of silence – silent daffodils, silent patients, a thrust singing, a dumb man speaking. The poem failed, draft after draft. At last I just told the story, setting the scene with three sentences of description. I chose every word carefully – the 'open-mouthed' afternoon, the sun 'treading' the path, the people 'observing' the silence of the flowers. 'Observing' has at least two meanings here. The woman 'in a cage' sat where the grid-pattern of sunlight fell, but her cage is also her illness.

Indoors the people were 'frozen' and silent. Outside the natural world was singing and dancing like 'flame'. We see, think and speak. We take this for granted, and the words within us meet the world outside and express our relationship with it. These ill people suffered from a disconnection between thought and language. The abyss within was more real to them than the beautiful world just outside their window.

To succeed, a poem needs a writer and a reader, a speaker and a listener. For one miraculous moment Walter listened, and he spoke. Language had done its healing work, and what was inside him, and the real, outside world of spring sunlight, daffodils, thrushes, lawn-mowers and people walking in the gardens, were reconnected through a poem.

Gillian Clarke

Anthology: Poems by Gillian Clarke _____

MY BOX

My box is made of golden oak,
my lover's gift to me.
He fitted hinges and a lock
of brass and a bright key.
He made it out of winter nights,
sanded and oiled and planed,
engraved inside the heavy lid
in brass, a golden tree.

In my box are twelve black books
where I have written down
how we have sanded, oiled and planed,
planted a garden, built a wall,
seen jays and goldcrests, rare red kites,
found the wild heartsease, drilled a well,
harvested apples and words and days
and planted a golden tree.

On an open shelf I keep my box.
Its key is in the lock.
I leave it there for you to read,
or them, when we are dead,
how everything is slowly made,
how slowly things made me,
a tree, a lover, words, a box,
books and a golden tree.

BABY-SITTING

I am sitting in a strange room listening
For the wrong baby. I don't love
This baby. She is sleeping a snuffly
Roseate, bubbling sleep; she is fair;
She is a perfectly acceptable child.
I am afraid of her. If she wakes
She will hate me. She will shout
Her hot midnight rage, her nose
Will stream disgustingly and the perfume
Of her breath will fail to enchant me.

To her I will represent absolute
Abandonment. For her it will be worse
Than for the lover cold in lonely
Sheets; worse than for the woman who waits
A moment to collect her dignity
Beside the bleached bone in the terminal ward.
As she rises sobbing from the monstrous land
Stretching for milk-familiar comforting,
She will find me and between us two
It will not come. It will not come.

MARGED

I think of her sometimes when I lie in bed,
falling asleep in the room I have made in the roof-space
over the old dark parlŵr where she died
alone in winter, ill and penniless.
Lighting the lamps, November afternoons,
a reading book, whisky gold in my glass.
At my type-writer tapping under stars
at my new roof-window, radio tunes
and dog for company. Or parking the car
where through the mud she called her single cow
up from the field, under the sycamore.
Or looking at the hills she looked at too.
I find her broken crocks, digging her garden.
What else do we share, but being women?

Marged is the name of the person who used to live in this house in
Wales before the writer came there. Parlŵr is Welsh for parlour.

105

Suggestions for assignments _____

1 Using the material in this unit, write a piece on Gillian Clarke, introducing her to new readers. Describe the sorts of things she chooses to write about, how she writes about them, and the kind of person she seems to be. Use extracts from the poems to show what you mean.

2 Write answers to these questions about the poems in the anthology:
My Box: What does the poem tell us about Gillian Clarke's life and what she values?
Baby-Sitting: The babysitter says 'I am afraid of her'. What makes her afraid?
Marged: Why is Gillian Clarke so interested in the person who used to live here before she did?

14

A Night-Piece
William Wordsworth

▷ It's night-time in a place like the one shown on p. 107, and the sky is overcast with clouds. There's a full moon, but you can only see it faintly through the clouds.

Write a description of that scene, using these words in your writing:

WHITENED   VEIL   INDISTINCTLY   DULL   LIGHT

▷ There is a traveller walking along the path, deep in thought. There is a break in the clouds, and the sudden brightness makes him look up.

Write a description of the scene, using these words:

GLEAM   STARTLES   UNOBSERVING   SPLIT   GLORY

▷ What does the traveller see as he continues looking up into the night sky?

MULTITUDES   WIND   UNFATHOMABLE   FAST   SILENT

Add a description of how the traveller feels when this moment has passed.

▷ Work your three descriptions into one piece of writing.

Read what other people have written. Choose the bits you like best to read to the rest of the group (or the whole of the class).

How have people used the words 'WHITENED', 'UNFATHOMABLE' and 'FAST'?

▷ What different ways have people used to describe the man's feelings at the end?

Which endings do you like best?

Write an ending together, as a class, using what you like best in each other's versions.

On 25 January 1798, William Wordsworth wrote a poem he called 'A Night-Piece'. He was writing about the scene you have just been recreating.

A NIGHT-PIECE

– The sky is overcast
With a continuous cloud of texture close,
Heavy and wan, all whitened by the Moon,
Which through that veil is indistinctly seen,
A dull, contracted circle, yielding light
So feebly spread that not a shadow falls,
Chequering the ground – from rock, plant, tree, or tower.
At length a pleasant instantaneous gleam
Startles the pensive traveller while he treads
His lonesome path, with unobserving eye
Bent earthwards; he looks up – the clouds are split
Asunder, – and above his head he sees
The clear Moon, and the glory of the heavens.
There in a black-blue vault she sails along,
Followed by multitudes of stars, that, small
And sharp, and bright, along the dark abyss
Drive as she drives: how fast they wheel away,
Yet vanish not! – The wind is in the trees,
But they are silent; – still they roll along
Immeasurably distant; and the vault,
Built round by those white clouds, enormous clouds,
Still deepens its unfathomable depth.
At length the Vision closes; and the mind,
Not undisturbed by the delight it feels,
Which slowly settles into peaceful calm,
Is left to muse upon the solemn scene.

▷ On a copy of the poem:

- Mark the four sections that match the four pieces of writing you did previously.

- Mark words that Wordsworth used that are like words that you have used. Has Wordsworth used them in the same way that you have?

- Mark any other parts of the poem that remind you of your own piece.

▷ The scene is a common one, and yet it seems unusual. Do you recognise what Wordsworth describes when he looks up?

▷
> At length the Vision closes; and the mind,
> Not undisturbed by the delight it feels,
> Which slowly settles into peaceful calm,
> Is left to muse upon the solemn scene.

Why did he choose the word 'Vision' rather than a word like 'sight' or 'episode'.
Describe in your own words what is happening in these four lines.

Wordsworth's sister, Dorothy, kept a journal in which she recorded her daily life, including the walks she shared with her brother in the Lake District. The journal was not private, and William and their friends read it. Here is an extract from the journal for 25 January 1798.

> *25th.* The sky spread over with one continuous cloud, whitened by the light of the moon, which, though her dim shape was seen, did not throw forth so strong a light as to chequer the earth with shadows. At once the clouds seemed to cleave asunder, and left her in the centre of a black-blue vault. She sailed along, followed by multitudes of stars, small, and bright, and sharp. Their brightness seemed concentrated, (half-moon).
>
> *(The Alfoxden Journal)*

▷ Match the extract against Wordsworth's poem. Is there anything that Dorothy writes which William does not use?

Anthology ———————————————

When we came to the foot of Brothers water I left William sitting on the Bridge and went along the path on the right side of the Lake through the wood. I was delighted with what I saw. The water under the boughs of the bare old trees, the simplicity of the mountains and the exquisite beauty of the path. There was one grey cottage. I repeated the Glowworm as I walked along. I hung over the gate, and thought I could have stayed for ever. When I returned I found William writing a poem descriptive of the sights and sounds we saw and heard. There was the gentle flowing of the stream, the glittering lively lake, green fields without a living creature to be seen on them, behind us, a flat pasture with 42 cattle feeding, to our left the road leading to the hamlet, no smoke there, the sun shone on the bare roofs. The people were at work ploughing, harrowing and sowing – lasses spreading dung, a dog's barking now and then, cocks crowing, birds twittering, the snow in patches at the top of the highest hills, yellow palms, purple and green twigs on the Birches, ashes with their glittering spikes quite bare. The hawthorn a bright green with black stems under the oak. The moss of the oak glossy. We then went on, passed two sisters at work, they first passed us, one with two pitch forks in her hand. The other had a spade. We had some talk with them. They laughed aloud after we were gone perhaps half in wantonness, half boldness. William finished his poem before we got to the foot of Kirkstone.

(*The Grasmere Journals*)

THE COCK IS CROWING

The cock is crowing,
The stream is flowing,
The small birds twitter,
The lake doth glitter,
The green field sleeps in the sun;
The oldest and youngest
Are at work with the strongest;
The cattle are grazing,
Their heads never raising;
There are forty feeding like one!
Like an army defeated
The snow hath retreated,
And now doth fare ill
On the top of the bare hill;
The Ploughboy is whooping – anon – anon:
There's joy in the mountains;
There's life in the fountains;
Small clouds are sailing,
Blue sky prevailing;
The rain is over and gone!

When we were in the woods beyond Gowborrow park we saw a few daffodils close to the water side. We fancied that the lake had floated the seeds ashore and that the little colony had so sprung up. But as we went along there were more and yet more and at last under the boughs of the trees, we saw that there was a long belt of them along the shore, about the breadth of a country turnpike road. I never saw daffodils so beautiful, they grew among the mossy stones about and about them, some rested their heads upon these stones as on a pillow for weariness and the rest tossed and reeled and danced and seemed as if they verily laughed with the wind that blew upon them over the lake, they looked so gay ever glancing ever changing. The wind blew directly over the lake to them. There was here and there a little knot and a few stragglers a few yards higher up but they were so few as not to disturb the simplicity and unity and life of that one busy highway. We rested again and again. The Bays were stormy, and we heard the waves at different distances and in the middle of the water like the sea.

(*The Grasmere Journals*)

DAFFODILS

I wandered lonely as a cloud
That floats on high o'er vales and hills,
When all at once I saw a crowd,
A host, of golden daffodils;
Beside the lake, beneath the trees,
Fluttering and dancing in the breeze.

Continuous as the stars that shine
And twinkle on the milky way,
They stretched in never-ending line
Along the margin of a bay:
Ten thousand saw I at a glance,
Tossing their heads in sprightly dance.

The waves beside them danced; but they
Out-did the sparkling waves in glee:
A poet could not but be gay,
In such a jocund company:
I gazed – and gazed – but little thought
What wealth the show to me had brought:

For oft, when on my couch I lie
In vacant or in pensive mood,
They flash upon that inward eye
Which is the bliss of solitude;
And then my heart with pleasure fills,
And dances with the daffodils.

Suggestions for assignments ──────────────

1 Many writers and artists make sketches of things they want to remember, and then work on them afterwards to produce a more polished version. William sometimes used Dorothy Wordsworth's journals as his 'notebook', as you have seen, and occasionally used her original words.

Keep a diary for a few days, particularly recording moments that you might want to write about. Record the details that will make the writing as vivid as possible, as Dorothy Wordsworth does. Choose days when you know you will be doing something interesting – going somewhere new, meeting someone and so on.

Leave it for a few days, and then reread the diary and choose one of the entries that you want to write about. Write a poem arising out of your diary entry. Keep all the drafts.

Write a final piece about the whole process. This will include:

- the journal

- the drafts

- the poem

- comments on how you came to write the poem

2 Consider the poems and the extracts from the journals in the anthology.

Write an essay explaining how the two seem to connect with each other and apparently influence each other. Give examples of words and phrases being used in both.

Do you think the poems were written by William, or by William and Dorothy?

15

One Art
Elizabeth Bishop

ONE ART

The art of losing isn't hard to master;
so many things seem filled with the intent
to be lost that their loss is no disaster.

Lose something every day. Accept the fluster
of lost door keys, the hours badly spent.
The art of losing isn't hard to master.

Then practise losing farther, losing faster:
places, and names, and where it was you meant
to travel. None of these will bring disaster.

I lost my mother's watch. And look! my last, or
next-to-last, of three loved houses went.
The art of losing isn't hard to master.

I lost two cities, lovely ones. And, vaster,
some realms I owned, two rivers, a continent.
I miss them, but it wasn't a disaster.

– Even losing you (the joking voice, a gesture
I love) I shan't have lied. It's evident
the art of losing's not too hard to master
though it may look (*Write* it!) like disaster.

▷ The poem talks about different kinds of loss. What kinds of thing have you lost?

▷ Mark in some way bits of the poem you find hard to understand. Talk about them with each other.

▷ In the poem, there are different kinds of loss, and the word 'lost' means different things. Make a copy of this table and work with someone else to complete the right-hand column.

▷ Use sentences or phrases and explore the meaning of 'lost' in each case.

THINGS LOST	'LOST' MEANS . . .
door keys	I can't find them
hours badly spent	
places, and names	
where it was you meant to travel	
my mother's watch	
three loved houses	
two cities, lovely ones	
some realms I owned	
you	

▷ How does the meaning of 'lost' change as you go through the poem?

▷ Is the person in the poem old or young? Does her age make a difference to the poem? Look especially at the last verse.
　　What led you to decide if she is young or old?

▷ How does the person in the poem feel about loss and losing? Do any of these statements describe how you think she feels?

- She feels sorry for herself.

- She accepts whatever happens in life.

- She has been hardened by experience, and is unmoved by loss now.

- She is more upset than she is prepared to say.

- She is wryly amused by what has happened to her.

- She is sad and resigned.

- She is lighthearted and casual.

Write your own piece about her feelings. What you write could include words or ideas from the statements above.

Anthology ────────────────────────────

RECUERDO

We were very tired, we were very merry –
We had gone back and forth all night on the ferry.
It was bare and bright, and smelled like a stable –
But we looked into a fire, we leaned across a table,
We lay on a hill-top underneath the moon;
And the whistles kept blowing, and the dawn came soon.

We were very tired, we were very merry –
We had gone back and forth all night on the ferry;
And you ate an apple, and I ate a pear,
From a dozen of each we had bought somewhere;
And the sky went wan, and the wind came cold,
And the sun rose dripping, a bucketful of gold.

We were very tired, we were very merry,
We had gone back and forth all night on the ferry.
We hailed, 'Good-morrow, mother!' to a shawl-covered
        head,
And bought a morning paper, which neither of us read;
And she wept, 'God bless you!' for the apples and the
        pears,
And we gave her all our money but our subway fares.

Edna St Vincent Millay

THE MUSHROOMER

Over the brow of the hill the mushroomer, walking,
Felt the wind playing with arrows of hidden frost,
Felt the air in his face like a steep cold river,
Felt the crying of lost

Lambs in his ears, and the airy ripple of wings.
Small wonder that he quite forgot his art
And, leaving his bucket empty, sat collecting these things
Instead, in his heart.

Colin Thiele

MY BOAT

My boat is being made to order. Right now it's about to leave
the hands of its builders. I've reserved a special place
for it down at the marina. It's going to have plenty of room
on it for all my friends: Richard, Bill, Chuck, Toby, Jim, Hayden,
Gary, George, Harold, Don, Dick, Scott, Geoffrey, Jack,
Paul, Jay, Morris, and Alfredo. All my friends! They know who
   they are.
Tess, of course. I wouldn't go anyplace without her.
And Kristina, Merry, Catherine, Diane, Sally, Annick, Pat,
   Judith, Susie, Lynne, Cindy, Jean, Mona.
Doug and Amy! They're family, but they're also my friends,
and they like a good time. There's room on my boat
for just about everyone. I'm serious about this!
There'll be a place on board for everyone's stories.
My own, but also the ones belonging to my friends.
Short stories, and the ones that go on and on. The true
and the made-up. The ones already finished, and the ones still
   being written.
Poems, too! Lyric poems, and the longer, darker narratives.
For my painter friends, paints and canvases will be on board
   my boat.
We'll have fried chicken, lunch meats, cheeses, rolls,
French bread. Every good thing that my friends and I like.
And a big basket of fruit, in case anyone wants fruit.
In case anyone wants to say he or she ate an apple,
or some grapes, on my boat. Whatever my friends want,
name it, and it'll be there. Soda pop of all kinds.
Beer and wine, sure. No one will be denied anything, on
   my boat.
We'll go out into the sunny harbor and have fun, that's the idea.
Just have a good time all around. Not thinking
about this or that or getting ahead or falling behind.
Fishing poles if anyone wants to fish. The fish are out there!
We may even go a little way down the coast, on my boat.
But nothing dangerous, nothing too serious.
The idea is simply to enjoy ourselves and not get scared.
We'll eat and drink and laugh a lot, on my boat.
I've always wanted to take at least one trip like this,
with my friends, on my boat. If we want to
we'll listen to Schumann on the CBC.
But if that doesn't work out, okay,
we'll switch to KRAB, The Who, and the Rolling Stones.

Whatever makes my friends happy! Maybe everyone
will have their own radio, on my boat. In any case,
we're going to have a big time. People are going to have fun,
and do what they want to do, on my boat.

Raymond Carver

DISPOSSESSED

This man is called Obed. His surname
is in another language. You do not need
to know it.

This is his room. He lives here
by himself. He does not have
enough food.

These are his wife and children.
They live a long way off. He sends them money.
They do not have enough food.

He goes home once a year. They run to meet him.
Sometimes they cry, we are told, for happiness.

He comes back to his room in the city
where they are not allowed. They stay
in the hard land where nothing grows.

Does this discourage him? Who knows? He throws
no bombs. He breaks no windows. He
sends home money.
          All his enterprise
is
   not forgetting.

Evangeline Paterson

Suggestions for assignments _____

1 Choose one of these ways of performing the poems in this unit.

- Work individually or with a partner to prepare a reading of one or more of the poems. You might finally tape record your reading.

- Work in a large group with all the poems in the unit. Decide the order in which the poems will be presented, and what part each person will play in the performance.

- If you have access to video equipment, you could produce a film of your performance. Pay attention to the backgrounds you have for the person speaking, to your choice of close-up or longer shot, and to the use of music and other images.

- Take one poem and produce alternative readings which express different moods and feelings. For instance, 'My Boat' could be bright and optimistic, or melancholy and despairing; 'Dispossessed' could be compassionate or dismissive.

2 All these poems express an 'Art of Living'. What advice does each of them offer you about making the best of life?

16

The Pilgrimage
George Herbert

▷ Many stories are constructed around the idea of a journey by land or sea, often including some kind of search or quest.

Make joint lists of stories and films in which journeys, explorations, voyages and quests are important. Include those stories you remember from when you were much younger.

▷ Places in stories can be friendly or dangerous, and some places are not what they seem.

Look back through the stories you collected, and make three lists:

- places which are threatening

- places which are safe or friendly

- places you can't be sure about, which could be either dangerous or friendly

▷ Think about your life as a kind of journey, beginning when you were born. Tell the story of your life so far in a quick sketch map.

Choose four or five significant times in your life journey, and decide how to represent them by drawing a place for each one. For example, would a sunny garden or a dark wood be the best way to picture your first day at your present school?

George Herbert was an aristocrat who could have become influential and famous, but who chose instead to be Rector of a small country parish. In the following poem, he describes his life as a kind of journey.

▷ What places has he chosen to represent important times in his life?

THE PILGRIMAGE

I travelled on, seeing the hill, where lay
   My expectation.
  A long it was and weary way.
  The gloomy cave of Desperation
I left on the one, and on the other side
   The rock of Pride.

And so I came to fancy's meadow strowed
   With many a flower:
  Fain would I here have made abode,
  But I was quickened by my hour.
So to care's copse I came, and there got through
   With much ado.

That led me to the wild of passion, which
   Some call the wold;
  A wasted place, but sometimes rich.
  Here I was robbed of all my gold,
Save one good Angel, which a friend had tied
   Close to my side.

At length I got unto the gladsome hill,
   Where lay my hope,
  Where lay my heart; and climbing still,
  When I had gained the brow and top,
A lake of brackish waters on the ground
   Was all I found.

With that abashed and struck with many a sting
   Of swarming fears,
  I fell and cried, Alas my King;
  Can both the way and end be tears?
Yet taking heart I rose, and then perceived
   I was deceived;

My hill was further: so I flung away,
   Yet heard a cry
  Just as I went, *None goes that way*
  And lives: If that be all, said I,
After so foul a journey death is fair,
   And but a chair.

This poem was published in 1633, and some words had other meanings then. One example is 'Angel', which was both a heavenly angel and a gold coin. Another example is 'chair'. A good dictionary will help you as you work on the poem.

▷ Draw a pictorial map of the journey in this poem. Begin at the bottom of the paper, and end at the top with the poet's final destination. Label the map with place names from the poem – for example, 'Rock of Pride'. Use colours, and include a human figure in each bit of your map.

   How will you show that the final destination cannot be seen for most of the journey?

▷ Work with someone else and produce a short statement which describes what George Herbert feels about Life and Death.

Anthology: Poems by George Herbert ———————

VERTUE

Sweet day, so cool, so calm, so bright,
The bridall of the earth and skie:
The dew shall weep thy fall to night;
      For thou must die.

Sweet rose, whose hue angrie and brave
Bids the rash gazer wipe his eye:
Thy root is ever in its grave,
      And thou must die.

Sweet spring, full of sweet dayes and roses,
A box where sweets compacted lie;
My musick shows ye have your closes,
      And all must die.

Onely a sweet and vertuous soul,
Like season'd timber, never gives;
But though the whole world turn to coal,
      Then chiefly lives.

THE CHURCH-FLOORE

Mark you the floore? that square and speckled stone,
    Which looks so firm and strong,
      Is *Patience:*

And th' other black and grave, wherewith each one
    Is checker'd all along,
      Humilitie:

The gentle rising, which on either hand
    Leads to the Quire above,
      Is *Confidence:*

But the sweet cement, which in one sure band
    Ties the whole frame, is *Love*
      And *Charitie.*

Hither sometimes Sinne steals, and stains
The marble's neat and curious veins:
But all is cleansed when the marble weeps.
    Sometimes Death, puffing at the doore,
    Blows all the dust about the floore:
But while he thinks to spoil the room, he sweeps.
    Blest be the *Architect*, whose art
    Could build so strong in a weak heart.

REDEMPTION

Having been tenant long to a rich Lord,
    Not thriving, I resolved to be bold,
    And make a suit unto him, to afford
A new small-rented lease, and cancell th' old.
In heaven at his manour I him sought:
    They told me there, that he was lately gone
    About some land, which he had dearly bought
Long since on earth, to take possession.
I straight return'd, and knowing his great birth,
    Sought him accordingly in great resorts;
    In cities, theatres, gardens, parks, and courts:
At length I heard a ragged noise and mirth
    Of theeves and murderers: there I him espied,
    Who straight, *Your suit is granted*, said, & died.

Suggestions for assignments ─────────────

1 Work with a partner to write a summary of each poem in two sentences. One should be in the form of a proverb, the other like a headline in a modern newspaper. Either sentence could use words out of the poems.

Exchange your statements with other pairs, and try to match their proverbs and headlines with the poems in the anthology.

Which is easier to relate to its original poem: the proverb or the headline?

2 Write a piece which explains which of the poems in the anthology is most like 'The Pilgrimage', and describes the different ways the poems picture Death. On the evidence of these poems, what can you say about George Herbert's beliefs in general?

One way you could write this is in the form of a statement by the poet to his readers, introducing himself and this selection of poems.

3 With a partner, make a study of the poems, looking for instance at

- the ways the poems rhyme

- the arrangement of lines in verses

- any other patterns you find

You might find it helpful to mark what you find on a photocopy of the poems.

Why did Herbert want his poems to have these patterns and structures?

17

A Poison Tree
William Blake

When you have read 'A Poison Tree' for the first time, write down immediately the first impressions you have, whatever they are. You don't have to write in an organised or coherent way. Just record the initial thoughts and feelings you have as soon as you have finished.

A POISON TREE

I was angry with my friend:
I told my wrath, my wrath did end.
I was angry with my foe:
I told it not, my wrath did grow.

And I water'd it in fears,
Night and morning with my tears;
And I sunned it with smiles,
And with soft deceitful wiles.

And it grew both day and night,
Till it bore an apple bright;
And my foe beheld it shine,
And he knew that it was mine,

And into my garden stole
When the night had veil'd the pole:
In the morning glad I see
My foe outstretch'd beneath the tree.

▷ Copy out the poem in pairs of lines. Write underneath each pair whatever the lines make you think of, or, if it seems appropriate, you could include sketches or other artwork. You could set it out like this:

> I was angry with my friend:
> I told my wrath, my wrath did end.

▷ Share what you have done with each other. When you have read other people's versions, write down any questions you have about the poem.

▷ What is your view on these ideas? Discuss them with other people.

- You should always express anger.
- It's wrong to be deceitful.
- Your enemy often has things you would like.
- Forgiveness is best.
- Evil things can look very attractive.
- Enemies deserve to be punished.
- It's good to get your own back.
- It's only natural to want revenge.

▷ Write a story, either based on real experience or invented, about a time when you were angry but didn't say so, and about what happened as a result.

THE SICK ROSE

O Rose, thou art sick.
The invisible worm
That flies in the night,
In the howling storm,

Has found out thy bed
Of crimson joy:
And his dark secret love
Does thy life destroy.

THE GARDEN OF LOVE

I went to the Garden of Love,
And saw what I never had seen:
A Chapel was built in the midst,
Where I used to play on the green.

And the gates of this Chapel were shut,
And 'Thou shalt not' writ over the door;
So I turn'd to the Garden of Love,
That so many sweet flowers bore;

And I saw it was filled with graves,
And tomb-stones where flowers should be;
And Priests in black gowns were walking their rounds,
And binding with briars my joys & desires.

LONDON

I wander thro' each charter'd street,
Near where the charter'd Thames does flow,
And mark in every face I meet
Marks of weakness, marks of woe.

In every cry of every Man,
In every Infant's cry of fear,
In every voice, in every ban,
The mind-forg'd manacles I hear.

How the Chimney-sweeper's cry
Every blackning Church appalls;
And the hapless Soldier's sigh
Runs in blood down Palace walls.

But most thro' midnights streets I hear
How the youthful Harlot's curse
Blasts the new-born Infant's tear,
And blights with plagues the Marriage hearse.

Suggestions for assignments _____

1 Work with a partner and read the poems in the anthology together.
Choose one of the poems and find ways of making a picture which
represents what you feel about it. (Blake's original poems were
accompanied by his own illustrations. You might like to look these up
in your library.)

2 Here are some of the titles from Blake's collected *Songs of Innocence
and Experience*:

Little Boy Lost
The Chimney Sweeper
Ah Sunflower
Infant Sorrow
The School Boy

Choose one of these and write your own piece – poem or prose – based
on the title. Reread the poems in this anthology first, and let your
writing be influenced by Blake's work.

18

The Poplar Field
William Cowper

T he poet is looking at a view he knows well, where poplars grew by the river. He remembers what it used to look like.

THE POPLAR FIELD

The poplars are felled; farewell to the shade,
And the whispering sound of the cool colonnade!
The winds play no longer and sing in the leaves,
Nor Ouse on his bosom their image receives.

Twelve years have elapsed since I first took a view
Of my favourite field, and the bank where they grew;
And now in the grass behold they are laid,
And the tree is my seat that once lent me a shade!

The blackbird has fled to another retreat,
Where the hazels afford him a screen from the heat,
And the scene where his melody charmed me before
Resounds with his sweet-flowing ditty no more.

▷ Make a copy of this table. Write in the boxes all that you can
discover about what the field used to be like and what it is like now.

The poplar field	As it was	As it is now
VERSE 1		
VERSE 2		
VERSE 3		

▷ There are two more verses to this poem. In them, the poet begins to
think about his own life.

In your group, suggest what the two verses might be about. Collect
the suggestions together, and decide which you think are the most
likely.

THE POPLAR FIELD

The poplars are felled; farewell to the shade,
And the whispering sound of the cool colonnade!
The winds play no longer and sing in the leaves,
Nor Ouse on his bosom their image receives.

Twelve years have elapsed since I first took a view
Of my favourite field, and the bank where they grew;
And now in the grass behold they are laid,
And the tree is my seat that once lent me a shade!

The blackbird has fled to another retreat,
Where the hazels afford him a screen from the heat,
And the scene where his melody charmed me before
Resounds with his sweet-flowing ditty no more.

My fugitive years are all hasting away,
And I must ere long lie as lowly as they,
With a turf on my breast, and a stone at my head,
Ere another such grove shall arise in its stead.

'Tis a sight to engage me, if anything can,
To muse on the perishing pleasures of man;
Though his life be a dream, his enjoyments, I see,
Have a being less durable even than he.

▷ Look back at the photograph of poplars on page 134. How
successfully does it illustrate the poem?

▷ Work in pairs, within a time limit of fifteen minutes. Set out to learn
by heart as much of the poem as you can.
  After the time is up, put the poem away and see how much of it
you can remember together.
  Which bits did you find particularly easy to remember?
  What is it about the bits you can remember that makes them easy
to learn?

PROPORTION

It is not growing like a tree
In bulke, doth make man better bee;
Or standing long an Oake, three hundred yeare,
To fall a logge at last, dry, bald, and seare:
A Lillie of a Day,
Is fairer farre, in May,
Although it fall, and die that night;
It was the Plant, and flowre of light.
In small proportions, we just beautie see:
And in short measures, life may perfect bee.

Ben Jonson

ON KILLING A TREE

It takes much time to kill a tree,
Not a simple jab of the knife
Will do it. It has grown
Slowly consuming the earth,
Rising out of it, feeding
Upon its crust, absorbing
Years of sunlight, air, water,
And out of its leprous hide
Sprouting leaves.

So hack and chop
But this alone won't do it.
Not so much pain will do it.
The bleeding bark will heal
And from close to the ground
Will rise curled green twigs,
Miniature boughs
Which if unchecked will expand again
To former size.

No,
The root is to be pulled out –
Out of the anchoring earth;
It is to be roped, tied,
And pulled out – snapped out
Or pulled out entirely,
Out from the earth-cave,
And the strength of the tree exposed,
The source, white and wet,
The most sensitive, hidden
For years inside the earth.

Then the matter
Of scorching and choking
In sun and air,
Browning, hardening,
Twisting, withering,

And then it is done.

Gieve Patel

SIC VITA*

Like to the falling of a Starre;
Or as the flights of Eagles are;
Or like the fresh springs gawdy hew;
Or silver drops of morning dew;
Or like a wind that chafes the flood;
Or bubbles which on water stood;
Even such is man, whose borrow'd light
Is streight call'd in, and paid to night.

The Wind blowes out; the Bubble dies;
The Spring entomb'd in Autumn lies;
The Dew dries up; the Starre is shot;
The Flight is past; and Man forgot.

Henry King

* 'Sic vita' is part of the Latin expression, 'sic vita
hominum est' which means 'such is men's life'   Cicero (Orationes)

RISING FIVE

'I'm rising five', he said,
'Not four', and little coils of hair
Un-clicked themselves upon his head.
His spectacles, brimful of eyes to stare
At me and the meadow, reflected cones of light
Above his toffee-buckled cheeks. He'd been alive
Fifty-six months or perhaps a week more:

                          not four,
But rising five.

Around him in the field the cells of spring
Bubbled and doubled; buds unbuttoned; shoot
And stem shook out the creases from their frills,
And every tree was swilled with green.
It was the season after blossoming,
Before the forming of the fruit;

                  not May.
But rising June.

          And in the sky
The dust dissected tangential light:

                    not day,
But rising night;
          not now,
But rising soon.

The new buds push the old leaves from the bough.
We drop our youth behind us like a boy
Throwing away his toffee-wrappers. We never see the flower,
But only the fruit in the flower; never the fruit,
But only the rot in the fruit. We look for the marriage bed
In the baby's cradle, we look for the grave in the bed:

                        not living,
But rising dead.

                        Norman Nicholson

Suggestions for assignments

1 Talk about the poems in the anthology, and compare them with Cowper's poem.

- Which of the poems do you think is most like 'The Poplar Field'? Do any of them seem to you to be completely different in meaning?

- Where would you place each of the poems along this line?

GLOOMY ◄──────────────────────► CHEERFUL

- 'The Poplar Field' rhymes in a straightforward way – each pair of lines rhymes, and all the lines are the same length. Look at the way the other poems are constructed, and see what patterns you can find.

2 Work in a group to produce a booklet which contains your presentation of four of the poems in this unit. You will need to decide on these points:

- which of the poems you will *not* choose

- the best order for the ones you use

- whether to include illustrations (drawings, photographs or reproductions). If you decide to use illustrations, share out the work of finding or producing them

- how to draft a commentary which links the poems, and explains your thoughts about them. Where will each piece of writing have most effect: before the poem it refers to, or after it?

- whether to include any biographical information about the poets

- how to present the pages – photocopies of the poems? or handwritten? or designed on a word processor?

- a title for the booklet, and a cover of your own design

3 Poems sometimes start from a feeling, sometimes a thought, sometimes a memory, sometimes an event. Consider what might have given the poets the idea for the poems in this anthology.
   You could write your ideas in one of these ways.

- Imagine yourself as the poet, telling the story of how the poem came to be written.

- Write an interview with two or more of the poets. What happens if you make the poets talk to each other?

- Write the notebook or journal entry the poet might have written about the starting point.

- Take each poem in turn and write some notes on the clues in it about what the starting point might have been.

19

A Roadside Feast
Peter Redgrove

A ROADSIDE FEAST

He slaps the hedgehog off the road
He chivvies it off with scraping prongs
He pins it alive on metal points
The blood catches the starlight
He says you must watch for fleas and not touch the vermin
He prods it down in the bank of clay
He stirs it round until it is an earth ball
Taking a twig he scrapes it off
Into the heart of the fire where it glows
And sizzles like a speeding cannonball
A high-pitched cry of juice from a blowhole
With his trowel he dibbles it out on a stone
Taps it and cracks it, the clay shards-off
He pulls them with scalding fingers
A roasting smell pays attention, we lean forward,
Like a six-inch pig the naked food
Glorious with grease. He waves us off
Bake your own hedge-pig, he says.
I pick up a shard, daggered with long pins.

▷ Work out in pairs precisely what happens to the hedgehog in the poem.
    Could you do what 'he' does?
    Why does 'he' do it?

▷ We watch what happens, but we don't seem to be told how 'I' feels.
    Work in small groups and complete this chart. Write in the appropriate quotation from the poem.

What happens	Quotation	What 'I' feels
When the blood comes		
When they hear the hedgehog baking		
When the clay comes off the baked hedgehog		
	Bake your own hedge-pig	
	I pick up a shard, daggered with long pins	

▷ Consider these alternative endings, and discuss what difference they would make to the poem.

1: The poem ends with the previous line:
    Bake your own hedge-pig, he says.

2: The poem ends with a new last line:
    I watch him eat, and turn away.

3: The poem ends with these two lines:
    I pick up a shard, daggered with long pins
    and the baked clay crumbles in my hand.

Anthology ———————————————————————

THE CRABS

There was a bucket full of them. They spilled,
crawled, climbed, clawed: slowly tossed
and fell: precision made: cold iodine color of their own
world of sand and occasional brown weed, round stone
chilled clean in the chopping waters of their coast.
One fell out. The marine thing on the grass
tried to trundle off, barbarian and immaculate and to be
    killed
with his kin. We lit water: dumped the living mass
in: contemplated tomatoes and corn: and with the good
    cheer of civilized man,
cigarettes, that is, and cold beer, and chatter,
waited out and lived down the ten-foot-away clatter
of crabs as they died for us inside their boiling can.

Richard Lattimore

THE TROUT

Flat on the bank I parted
Rushes to ease my hands
In the water without a ripple
And tilt them slowly downstream
To where he lay, light as a leaf,
In his fluid sensual dream.

Bodiless lord of creation
I hung briefly above him
Savouring my own absence
Senses expanding in the slow
Motion, the photographic calm
That grows before action.

As the curve of my hands
Swung under his body
He surged, with visible pleasure.
I was so preternaturally close
I could count every stipple
But still cast no shadow, until

144

The two palms crossed in a cage
Under the lightly pulsing gills.
Then (entering my own enlarged
Shape, which rode on the water)
I gripped. To this day I can
Taste his terror in my hands.

John Montague

FINDING A SHEEP'S SKULL

Sudden shock of bone
at the path's edge,
like a larger mushroom
almost hidden by leaves.

I handle the skull gently
shaking out earth and spiders.
Loose teeth chock in the jaw:
it smells of nothing.

I hold it up to sunlight,
a grey-green translucent shell.
Light pours in
            like water
through blades and wafers of bone.
       In secret caves
filaments of skull hang down;
frost and rain have worked
            to shredded lace.

The seasons waste its symmetry.
       It is a cathedral
echoing spring; in its decay
            plainsong of lamb
            and field and sun
inhabits bone.

The shallow cranium
fits in my palm

– for speculative children
I bring it home.

Frances Horovitz

Suggestions for assignments

1 How does each of the anthology poems remind you of 'Roadside Feast'?

2 Choose one of these suggestions to work on:

Roadside Feast: Write a piece which explains the title, and either says why the poem is worth reading or why no one else should read it.
The Crabs: Imagine you are watching this scene. When you feel familiar enough with the poem, describe what you, the watcher, can see, and what you feel. Do this without referring back to the poem so that you will be describing what you think rather than just summarising the poem itself.
The Trout: Choose a few phrases from the poem which you want to write about. Write each phrase and then an explanation of why it interests you.
Finding a Sheep's Skull: Have you found some relic of a creature? Tell your story about it.

20

Travelling Through the Dark
William Stafford

TRAVELLING THROUGH
THE DARK

Travelling through the dark I found a deer
dead on the edge of the Wilson River road.
It is usually best to roll them into the canyon:
that road is narrow; to swerve might make more dead.

By glow of the tail-light I stumbled back of the car
and stood by the heap, a doe, a recent killing;
she had stiffened already, almost cold.
I dragged her off; she was large in the belly.

My fingers touching her side brought me the reason –
her side was warm; her fawn lay there waiting,
alive, still, never to be born.
Beside that mountain road I hesitated.

The car aimed ahead its lowered parking lights;
under the hood purred the steady engine.
I stood in the glare of the warm exhaust turning red;
around our group I could hear the wilderness listen.

I thought hard for us all – my only swerving –
then pushed her over the edge into the river.

▷ Do you see pictures when you read? Some people think they see moving pictures, some see still pictures; others say they don't see any pictures at the time, but when they think about it afterwards, they do.

   What happens when you and your friends read this poem? Do you see pictures?

▷ Trying to picture this poem is trying to understand it. One way of picturing is creating a storyboard, that is a script for a film or television programme.

   A storyboard gives an indication of what images might be used, any voice over, and any music or other sound effects. Lay it out like this.

IMAGE	V/O	FX

Produce a storyboard that could be used in the making of a video of this poem. Begin with the title frame, try to use between ten and fifteen frames, and indicate camera angles, close-ups and long shots. Don't bother about producing beautiful drawings. What matters is that your image should show what you think is most important.

▷ How many people are in your video?
   What was your most important close-up?
   Which were the silent moments in your storyboard?
   Which parts couldn't you make pictures for? Which words or lines of the poem did you have to leave out?

▷ What different endings for the film have been suggested in your group?

   Most films wouldn't end where the poem ends. Some possible endings in a film would be:

- The car drives away, silence returns. The camera focuses on the river, and zooms in slowly on the body of the deer.

- We see a close-up of the man. The camera pulls further and further back until he seems just a dot in the landscape in the lights of the car.

- The driver gets back into the car and drives away. We follow and see close-ups of the expression on his face. Then the car drives away from us and we see its tail lights disappearing into the night.

But a film could also end the same way the poem does:

- We see the man push the deer over and the screen goes blank and silent.

Write a description of what you think would be the best way to end the film.

▷   I thought hard for us all – my only swerving –
         then pushed her over the edge into the river.

What is there to think about?

ENEMY ENCOUNTER

for Lilac

Dumping (left over from the autumn)
Dead leaves, near a culvert
I come on
           a British Army Soldier
With a rifle and a radio
Perched hiding. He has red hair.

He is young enough to be my weenie
-bopper daughter's boy-friend.
He is like a lonely little winter robin.

We are that close to each other, I
Can nearly hear his heart beating.

I say something bland to make him grin,
But his glass eyes look past my side
-whiskers down
           the Shore Road street.
I am an Irish man
           and he is afraid
That I have come to kill him.

Padraic Fiacc

INTERRUPTION TO
A JOURNEY

The hare we had run over
Bounced about the road
On the springing curve
Of its spine.

Cornfields breathed in the darkness,
We were going through the darkness and
The breathing cornfields from one
Important place to another.

We broke the hare's neck
And made that place, for a moment,
The most important place there was,
Where a bowstring was cut
And a bow broken forever
That had shot itself through so many
Darknesses and cornfields.

It was left in that landscape.
It left us in another.

Norman MacCaig

MOUSE'S NEST

I found a ball of grass among the hay
And progged it as I passed and went away;
And when I looked I fancied something stirred,
And turned agen and hoped to catch the bird –
When out an old mouse bolted in the wheats
With all her young ones hanging at her teats;
She looked so odd and so grotesque to me,
I ran and wondered what the thing could be,
And pushed the knapweed bunches where I stood;
Then the mouse hurried from the craking brood.
The young ones squeaked, and as I went away
She found her nest again among the hay.
The water o'er the pebbles scarce could run
And broad old cesspools glittered in the sun.

John Clare

Suggestions for assignments ⎯⎯⎯⎯⎯⎯⎯⎯⎯

1 The poems show a series of encounters which 'make that place for a moment the most important place there was'. The meetings are unexpected, pass quickly, but live in the mind.

Write your own piece, based on a real experience, or make one up. Decide who is meeting who or what, where they are, and what happens.

2 Consider the last two lines of the three poems in the anthology. Picture them in any way you wish, artwork as well as storyboard, sketch or diagram.

Write a commentary on your work, in which you explain your thinking, and also what your picturing cannot show. Describe what it was in the poems that made you come to your decisions.

The work you have already done on 'Travelling Through the Dark' could be added to this assignment.